Irving Elting

**Dutch Village Communities on the Hudson River**

Irving Elting

**Dutch Village Communities on the Hudson River**

ISBN/EAN: 9783337233136

Printed in Europe, USA, Canada, Australia, Japan

Cover: Foto ©Suzi / pixelio.de

More available books at **www.hansebooks.com**

# JOHNS HOPKINS UNIVERSITY STUDIES

## IN

## HISTORICAL AND POLITICAL SCIENCE

### HERBERT B. ADAMS, Editor.

---

History is past Politics and Politics present History — *Freeman*

---

## FOURTH SERIES

## I

# Dutch Village Communities

### ON THE

# HUDSON RIVER

### BY IRVING ELTING, A. B.

---

### BALTIMORE

N. MURRAY, PUBLICATION AGENT, JOHNS HOPKINS UNIVERSITY

### JANUARY, 1886

JOHN MURPHY & CO., PRINTERS,
BALTIMORE.

# DUTCH VILLAGE COMMUNITIES

ON THE

# HUDSON RIVER.[1]

No two rivers have been oftener compared than the Rhine and the Hudson, and the latter has sometimes been termed the "Rhine of America." In interest, in importance, and in beautiful scenery, they have much in common. Yet the comparisons between them, likely to be made by travellers, are chiefly of difference rather than of likeness. The Rhine which, rising in the Alps, pushes its way between France and Germany, through the Netherlands and, with divided channel, out into the Northern Sea, is a narrower, swifter running, more tortuous stream than the Hudson, which in fact is, in its later course, not properly a river but a fjord—an inlet of the sea—with one hundred and fifty miles of tide-water ebbing and flowing in a broader bed, and between higher mountains, than the Rhine can boast. The Rhine is famous for its castle-crowned hills, illustrating with their ruins an historical tale begun in the time of Cæsar. About the Hudson, our own Washington Irving has thrown a grace-

---

[1] In the preparation of this paper much of the material has been gleaned from records in County Clerks' offices, but special acknowledgments are due to the writings of Laveleye, Sir Henry Maine, J. R. Green, Dr. O'Callaghan, Mr. Brodhead, and Gen. J. Watts de Peyster; also to the assistance, generously rendered in the loan of books, documents, and MSS., by Mr. Samuel Burhans of New York, by the officers of the Huguenot Bank, the Rev. Ame Vennema, Messrs. Jacob Elting and Edmund Eltinge of New Paltz, and by Messrs. Wallace Bruce, C. B. Herrick, and Frank Hasbrouck of Pough-keepsie.

ful mantle of later romance and legend, and in variety and grandeur of natural scenery, the "Rhine of America" surpasses her foreign sister.

Between these two rivers, there exists, unnoticed by the traveller, and unnoted, for the most part, even by the historian, a bond of union formed by the institutional relationship of the village communities which have had their existence, with similar customs, similar laws, and similar forms of government, upon the banks of each stream.

It is only within a comparatively few years that, by reason of the researches of Von Maurer, Sir Henry Maine, and Laveleye, the term "village community" has gained a special and instructive significance for the student of institutional history. It has come to represent a civil unit, universal to all peoples—at least to those of Aryan stock—at a certain stage of the progress in civilization; with collective property or ownership of land in common, and with a representative governing body chosen by, and from, the co-owners of the domain, to administer the common affairs, as its distinctive characteristics. Absolute and individual rights in land, as we know them, Von Maurer and his followers assert to be of recent origin; separate property, they say, has grown, by a series of changes, out of common or collective ownership.[1]

---

[1] The writer of this paper states this theory of the origin and growth of property rights among the Aryan peoples, because it is held by the majority of students who have given their attention to the subject; but he is not unmindful of the fact that the pains-taking and scholarly researches of his friend Dr. Denman W. Ross in America, and the investigations of others, *e. g.* Fustel de Coulanges, in Europe, have led them to oppose the view taken by Sir Henry Maine and to maintain that separate individual ownership *preceded* the various forms of ownership in common. A decision of this question, if it were possible, is not necessary for the present purpose of examining the village communities on the Hudson River. Whether or not the distribution of common lands among the primitive Germanic tribes was originally *per stirpes* and not *per capita,*—was, in short, collective tenure and not communism,—the local institutions of the Dutch villages in New York can hardly fail to impress the disciple of either theory with the closeness, and consequent importance, of the relationship of Old World and New World types of government.

Nowhere does this development of property rights in their successive forms exhibit itself more clearly than among the Germanic tribes which the Romans first met as pastoral groups moving from place to place, and subsisting upon the results of the chase, or upon the cattle which they herded on the common lands where they chanced to be. In this stage of race development there is essentially no holding of landed property, not even in common. That comes when the pastoral period is succeeded by the agricultural. The tillage of the soil brings with it ownership of land, but in the first instance a *common* ownership. The pastoral habits clung to the tribes, and they moved about, cultivating fresh lands of the unoccupied territory each year.[1] As the agricultural system became more important, the village community crystallized. The territory of the tribe was the Mark, in which each family was entitled to the temporary enjoyment of a share.[2] The woodland and pasturage were entirely common, and so continued even after the arable land had, in the progress towards individual property, been allotted and rendered subject to hereditary rights. Cæsar and Tacitus testify to the existence of the peculiar features of the village community among the Germanic tribes of the Rhine countries.[3] Laveleye asserts that " the triennial rotation of crops was introduced into Germany, . . . before the time of Charlemagne."[4] . . . " The parcels in each field had to be tilled at the same time, devoted to the same crops, and abandoned to the common pasture at the same period, according to the rule of *Flurzwang*, or compulsory rotation. The inhabitants assembled to deliberate on all that concerned the cultivation, and to determine the order and time of the various agricultural

---

[1] Laveleye, Primitive Property, p. 102.

[2] Laveleye, Primitive Property, p. 105.

[3] Laveleye, Primitive Property, p. 105 (Citing De Bel. Gal. L. VI. c. 29, and Tac. Germ. c. VII).

[4] Laveleye, Primitive Property, p. 110.

operations.[1] The member of the German village community was a *free man* in the best sense of the word; he had a share in the common property, he had a voice in the assembly of his equals, and was subject to no arbitrary ruler. It is not strange that groups of these freemen were able to make themselves masters of the empire of the Cæsars.

Yet their very power had in it the seeds of its own destruction. The force of the combined freemen of the tribe or canton led to conquest over other tribes; conquest led to the acquisition of the territory of the conquered, and this in turn resulted in that unequal division of the acquired territory, the outcome of which was the feudal system. The leader of the band of freemen became the most important personage in the group; equality ceased to exist: the chief took the largest portion of the new land, and gave it out in parcels to his under-companions in arms, thus becoming, in time, the lord of the manor, subject indeed to his king,—the sovereign of the whole territory,—but having within his own manor arbitrary rule, and having under him and subject to his entire control, men who, in early Germanic times, would have been his equals.

Thus at the end of the tenth century in western Europe, but especially in France, the conditions of society were in many respects the very opposite of those by means of which the primitive German village community fostered the principles of freedom, equality, and representative government. The voice of the people in government had practically ceased to be heard. "Land has become the sacramental tie of all public relations; the poor man depends upon the rich, not as his chosen patron, but as the owner of the land he cultivates, the lord of the court to which he does suit and service, the leader whom he is bound to follow to the host."[2]

The earlier, freer, community-life, however, with the customs of common land tenure and of government by freemen

---

[1] Laveleye, Primitive Property, p. 111.
[2] Stubbs' Constitutional History, I, p. 167.

met in general assembly, survived the changes just described, in some of the more secluded portions of the country, notably in the forest regions of the lower Palatinate east of the Rhine, [1] and in those northern provinces of the Netherlands— Friesland, Groningen and Drenthe—whose free peoples Rome never conquered, and whose right of self-government no haughty baron ever suppressed. Throughout the Netherlands, in fact, the feudal system, though prevailing, never obtained the firm foothold it gained in France, and even in more distant England. The industrial spirit and the growth of the importance of towns among the Dutch had modified the feudal system in Holland in a marked degree.[2] "Holland was an aggregate of towns each providing for its own defence, administering its own finances, and governing itself by its own laws."[3] Each town was governed by "a 'Wethouderschap' or Board of Magistrates, consisting of several burgomasters [4] and a certain number of Schepens or Aldermen."[5] The term of office was usually annual. The burgomasters and schepens were chosen by the eight or nine "goodmen" who were "elected by the 'Vroedschap,'[6] or great council of the town, which was itself composed, in most cases, of all the inhabitants who possessed a certain property qualification. There was also another important officer, named the 'schout,' who, in early times, was appointed by the Count, out of a triple nomination by the wethouders. The functions of the schout—whose name, according to Grotius, was

---

[1] Dr. H. B. Adams, in "The Germanic Origin of New England Towns," Vol. I of this series, pp. 13, 14, describes the primitive character of the villages now to be found in the Odenwald and Black Forest.

[2] Brodhead's History of the State of New York, 1609–1664, p. 192.

[3] Brodhead's History of the State of New York, p. 453.

[4] This privilege of "burgher-recht," which had to be acquired to entitle a resident to every municipal franchise, introduced some inequality among the people.

[5] Brodhead's History of the State of New York, pp. 453-4.

[6] Motley, Dutch Republic, I, p. 37, mentions the "Vroedschappen" or councillors.

an abbreviation of 'schuld-rechter,' or a judge of crimes—
were somewhat analagous to those of bailiff or county sheriff;
combining, however, with them some of the duties of a prose-
cuting attorney."[1]

In the course of the fifteenth century "the inhabitants
were authorized . . . to select from among themselves a certain number, double or triple, from which the head of the
government elected and appointed such as it considered best
qualified to act as 'schepens' or magistrates."[2]

As early as 1295 the "Tribunal of Well-born Men," or of
"Men's Men," as it was sometimes called, was instituted in
the Low Countries. It originally had separate criminal and
civil jurisdiction. Afterwards the Courts were united, and
the bailiff of each district was allowed to administer justice
in both civil and criminal cases with "Thirteen elected good
Men." This tribunal, which resembled the modern jury, continued until the spring of 1614, when the number was altered
to "Nine Well-born Men" who administered justice together.[3]

"The States-General," says Brodhead, "was, in one sense,
an aggregate assembly of the States of the provinces, each of
which might send an unlimited number of deputies."[4]

"The sovereign power of the province did not, however,
reside in the States of Holland, but in the constituencies of

---

[1] Brodhead, *supra*, pp. 453–4.

[2] O'Callaghan, History of New Netherland, I., p. 391.

[3] O'Callaghan, History of New Netherland, II., p. 40.

In view of the foregoing statements relating to early town government
in the Rhine Countries, the position taken by Palfrey in his History of New
England seems surprising. In Vol. I., pp. 275–6, he says: "The institution of towns had its origin in Massachusetts, and was borrowed thence by
the other governments." He speaks of the selectmen as if they were indi-
genous to New England, whereas they are found to be as old as the history
of Germanic institutions. Certainly, if the ancestors of our Hudson River
settlers had, in Holland, chosen their selectmen, varying in number from
thirteen to eight, from a time as early as the thirteenth century and probably much earlier, their Dutch descendants did not need to borrow from
Massachusetts "the institution of towns."

[4] Brodhead's History of the State of New York, pp. 454–5.

the deputies. The real authorities were the college of nobles, and the municipal councils of the towns. To them each deputy was responsible for his vote, and under their instructions alone he acted. Thus the government of Holland, in fact, rested mainly upon its people."[1] In 1477, the first assembly of the States-General resulted in a charter of liberties, which after successive demands by the towns, "guaranteed and confirmed the ancient privileges of the municipal governments, and recognized the right of the towns, at all times, to confer with each other, and with the States of the Netherlands. It declared that no taxes should be imposed without the consent of the States; and it distinctly secured the freedom of trade and commerce.[2] Thus at the close of the sixteenth century, the liberty-loving Netherlanders had not only preserved much of the freedom of the people, which the feudal system had tended to crush out, but they had also adhered to a freedom of trade which brought them wealth, and made them the most important maritime country of the world.

Just at this time—the beginning of the seventeenth century—the enterprising East India Company sent out from Amsterdam a small vessel under command of an English sailor to discover, if possible, a northwest passage to India. So it happened that in the fall of 1609,—nearly a dozen years before the Mayflower landed at Plymouth,—Hendrick Hudson, in his Dutch vessel the "Half Moon," sailed into the mouth of the river which now bears his name. Five years later the States-General of Holland granted a charter to the United New Netherland Company, giving it exclusive trade within the territory to which Holland considered that Hudson's discovery entitled her. Its object was not colonization and improvement of the land, but the monopoly of the fur-trade with the Indians. Three trading posts were established on the river, at what is now New York, at Albany, and at

[1] Brodhead's History of the State of New York, p. 452.

[2] Brodhead's History of the State of New York, p. 437.

Rondout,—the mouth of the river, the head of navigation, and about midway between the two.

The charter of the first company expired in 1618, and in 1621 the States-General granted another to the West India Company, with the monopoly of exclusive trade as before. The general government of the company was lodged in a board or assembly of nineteen delegates. They might choose a Director-General and Council who " were invested with all powers, judicial, legislative and executive, but the resolutions and customs of Fatherland were to be received as the paramount rule of action."[1]

In 1624, in the same ship with Peter Minuit,—the first Director-General of the West India Company,—there came to New Netherland some families of Walloons from the frontier of Belgium and France. After a temporary settlement on Staten Island, they removed to the north-western extremity of Long Island on a bay called the " Wahle-Bocht," or " the bay of the foreigners," where they established a permanent home. With the exception of such small accessions, comparatively nothing was done towards advancing settlement and agriculture during the seven years which followed the incorporation of the West India Company. The States-General, accordingly, determined to plant " colonies " or seignorial fiefs, or manors, in the new country, and in June, 1629, ratified the document called " Freedoms and Exemptions," granted by the Assembly of XIX of the West India Company, " to all such as shall plant any colonies in New Netherland." This charter established a monopoly in land, as the previous one had in trade, and put the valley of the Hudson largely into the hands of proprietors who were favorites of the company. Each proprietor or " Patroon " was to undertake to plant a colony of fifty souls, upwards of fifteen years old, and for that purpose might extend his limits four (that is sixteen English) miles on one side of the river, or half that

---

[1] O'Callaghan, History of New Netherland, I., p. 90.

distance on both sides, "and so far into the country as the situation of the occupiers will permit."[1] The company was to retain the intervening lands, and no one was allowed to come within thirty miles distance without the consent of the "Patroon;" subject, however, to the order of the commander and council. The Patroons were to hold the lands "as a perpetual inheritance," establish officers and magistrates in the cities, and dispose of their property by will. The colonists were to be freed by the company from payment of customs, taxes, excise, or other contributions, for the space of ten years, after which they should pay the usual exactions. The most liberal clause of the charter is the one which grants to other persons, who should go and settle there, but without the privileges of the Patroons, as much land (with the approbation of the Director-General and Council) "as they shall be able properly to improve."[2]

The Patroons and colonists were to endeavor to support a minister and a schoolmaster, that thus the service of God and the zeal for religion may not grow cool, and be neglected among them; and that they do, for the first, procure a comforter of the sick there."[3] But the colonists were prohibited from manufacturing, "on pain of being banished, and as perjurers to be arbitrarily punished." The Patroons were entitled to the services of the colonists, and were to be supplied with "blacks" by the company. Thus the feudal tenure of Europe, in a somewhat modified form, but conferring less liberty than the Dutch had enjoyed in the Fatherland, was imposed upon the settlers of the Hudson river valley by the States-General of Holland acting under the instigation of the Assembly of XIX. of the West India Company. "While it secured the right of the Indian to the soil and enjoined

---

[1] O'Callaghan, History of New Netherland, I., p. 113. (Citing Hol. Doc. ii., pp. 98, 99.

[2] O'Callaghan, History of New Netherland, I., p. 118.

[3] O'Callaghan, History of New Netherland, I., p. 119.

schools and churches, it scattered the seeds of servitude, slavery and aristocracy.  While it gave to freemen as much land as they could cultivate, and exempted colonists from taxation for ten years, it fettered agriculture by restricting commerce and prohibiting manufactures." [1]

Kilien Van Rensselaer, a merchant of Amsterdam and one of the directors of the West India Company, became a Patroon in 1630 under this " Freedoms and Exemptions " charter of 1629, and secured the grant of a large tract of land on both sides of the Hudson, including the present site of Albany.  As Patroon he was " empowered to administer civil and criminal justice in person or by deputy within his colonie, to appoint local officers and magistrates ; to erect courts and to take cognizance of all crimes committed within his limits." [2]

Nominally an appeal lay from the manorial courts to the Director-General and Council at Fort Amsterdam, in cases

---

[1] Moulton, History of New York, pp. 387, 388.

It should be especially noted that in this earliest charter of 1629, notwithstanding its restriction of civil liberties, the Dutch recognized the prime importance of establishing in their colony here the foundations of religion and education.  So intimately were the two connected that, as Dr. Baird mentions in his " Huguenot Emigration to America" (Vol. I., p. 185), in 1656 some colonists set sail for New Nethsrlands in three ships, one of which carried a schoolmaster who was to be also " a comforter of the sick," till the minister arrived.  As early as 1633, Everardus Bogardus, the first minister in New Amsterdam, and Adam Roelandsen, the schoolmaster, came over from Holland together.—(Brodhead, p. 223).

Of the character and influence of the religious life of the Hudson river colonists, something will be said in connection with the account of New Paltz, which in most respects may be called the typical village community of the Hudson river.

The part which Dutch influence played in shaping the educational life of America, has not been given the general recognition it deserves.  Our free public school system, of which we are so justly proud, seems to have its beginnings distinctly traceable to the earliest life of the Dutch colonies

[2] O'Callaghan, History of New Netherland, I., p. 320.

(For Van Rensselaer Patent, see Docs. relating to Colonial Hist. N. Y., Vol. I., p. 44).

affecting life or limb, or where the amount in controversy was over twenty dollars ; but this right to appeal was rendered for the most part nugatory, by the exaction of a promise from the colonist at the time of settlement, that he would not resort to the higher tribunal. Thus, besides being subject to the laws prevailing elsewhere in New Netherland,—the civil code, the ordinances of the Province of Holland and of the United Netherlands, the edicts of the West India Company and of the Director and Council at Manhattan,—the colonists of the manor were also subject to such laws as the Patroon or his deputies might establish.[1] "Theoretically," says Mr. Brodhead, "the Patroon was always present in his court baron.[2] Practically, the government of the colony was administered by a court composed of two commissaries and two schepens, assisted by the colonial secretary and the schout."[3] The Patroon bore the expenses of preparing the land for occupancy. He set off farms, erected farm buildings, stocked them with tools and cattle, and so brought the farmer to his

---

here in America, and to have had its prototype in "the free schools in which," says Dr. Storrs (American Spirit and the Genesis of It, p. 47), "Holland had led the van of the world." Mr. Motley, in a letter to the St. Nicholas Society (cited by Dr. Storrs, *supra*), intimates that the New England colonists gained their educational impulses more from the Netherlands than from their own country. "It is very pleasant to reflect," he says, "that the New England pilgrims, during their residence in the glorious country of your ancestry, found already established there a system of schools which John of Nassau, eldest brother of William the Silent, had recommended in these words : 'You must urge upon the States-General that they should establish free schools, where children of quality as well as of poor families, for a very small sum, could be well and Christianly educated and brought up. This would be the greatest and most useful work you could ever accomplish for God and Christianity, and for the Netherlands themselves.' . . . This was the feeling about popular education in the Netherlands during the 16th century." In New Amsterdam in 1647, the Nine Men approved arrangements "for finishing the church and *reorganizing* the public schools."—(Brodhead, Hist. N. Y., p. 476).

[1] Brodhead's Hist. of N. Y., p. 305; O'Callaghan's Hist. of N. Y., p. 321.
[2] "Studies" I., VII, Old Maryland Manors, pp. 11, 12.
[3] Brodhead's Hist. of N. Y., p. 305.

work unhampered by want of capital. In return for these
outlays the civil code gave the Patroon many of the rights
incident to lordship under the feudal system. He was not
only entitled to the rent [1] fixed upon, but also to a portion of
the increase of the stock and of the produce of the farm.
Even to the remainder he had pre-emptive right, and the
farmer was not at liberty to sell any of his produce elsewhere,
until it had been refused by the Patroon. He required each
colonist to grind all grain at his mill, to obtain license from
him to fish or hunt within the domain, and as "lord of the
manor," he was the legal heir of all who died intestate within
the "colonie." [2]

This manor, thus early created under Dutch rule, [3] may
stand as a type of the later ones, most of which were established after the English obtained possession of the territory,
and before the close of the 17th century. The proprietary
on the Hudson river, therefore, had the power of establishing
the feudal system as they had in Maryland, where, as Mr.
Geo. Wm. Brown has stated, "express provision was made
for manors, lords of manors and manorial courts." [4]

In the patent for the Livingston manor given under the
hand and seal of Gov. Dongan, July 22, 1686, provision is
made for constituting "in the said Lordship and Mannor one
Court Leet and one Court Baron [5] . . . to be kept by the
said Robert Livingston his Heirs and assignes for ever or
theire or any of theire Stewards Deputed and appointed with

---

[1] The rent was usually paid in kind on the Hudson as it was in "Old
Maryland Manors." See "Studies," I., VII., p. 10.

[2] Brodhead's Hist. of N. Y., p. 305; O'Callaghan's Hist. of New Netherland, I., pp. 325–6.

[3] The summary above is from the Charter of Rensselaerswyck. In 1646,
Kieft's manorial grant to Van der Donck was of territory on which Yonkers
is now the chief town.

[4] Geo. Wm. Brown, The Origin and Growth of Civil Liberty in Maryland
(1850), p. 7. Conf. Maine, Village Communities, pp. 139, 140.

[5] "The ownership of the manorial estate carried with it in New York the
right to hold two courts," as Mr. Johnson says it did in Maryland—
"Studies," *supra*, p. 11.

full and ample Power and authority to Destraine for the
Rents Services and other Sumes of Mony Payable by Reason
of the Premises and all other Lawfull Remedyes and meanes
for the haveing . . . and Enjoyeing the Premissesse and
every parte and Parcell of the same and all Wasts Estrayes
Wrecks Deodands Goods of felons happening and being for-
feited within the said Lordshipp and Mannor,"[1] together
with the right of advowson and other incidents of feudal tenure, in which these Hudson river domains of the Patroons
were closely allied to the "Old Maryland Manors" as set
forth in Mr. Johnson's interesting monograph.[2]

So distasteful, to the Dutch settlers who had enjoyed a
greater freedom in the Fatherland, were these restrictions of
the manors, that the settlements did not rapidly increase.[3]
The beginnings of governmental life on the Hudson river,
therefore, were unfortunate for the growth of free institutions.
Monopoly—in trade, in land,[4] and in government—seemed to
be the foundation on which the settlers in New Netherland
must build their state.[5]

---

[1] Docs. Relating to Col. Hist. of N. Y., III., pp. 375–6.

[2] "Studies," *supra.*

[3] Evidence of the unpopularity of the manor government may be found
in a letter written by the Earl of Bellomont to the Lords of Trade, dated,
"New Yorke, Jan^y 2^d 1700/1." He says: "Mr. Livingston has on his
great grant of 16 miles long and 24 broad but 4 or 5 cottagers, as I am told,
men that live in vassallage under him and work for him and are too poor to
be farmers having not wherewithall to buy Cattle to stock a farm. Collonel
Courtland has also on his great grants 4 or 5 of these poor families;" other
like cases being mentioned.

[4] In the same letter he adds: "I believe there are not less than seven
millions of acres granted away in 13 grants, and all of them uninhabited
. . . except M^r Ranslaer's grant, which is 24 miles square, and on which
the town of Albany stands."—Docs. relating to the Hist. of N. Y., IV.,
pp. 822–3.

[5] The opinion, here expressed, that the manor system on the Hudson river
hampered the early development of representative government, may seem
to be inconsistent with Mr. Johnson's statement (Old Maryland Manors,
*supra,* p. 20) that, "it should not be thought that the aristocratic character

No Dutch village community seemed likely to rise under the first charter of 1629, and the need of inducing settlers to colonize New Netherland for agricultural purposes convinced the States-General of Holland that the monopoly they had unwisely established must, to some extent, be broken. In 1638 trade was taken from the exclusive privileges of the West India Company and made free. In 1640 there was granted a more liberal charter,[1] by which any one who should go to New Netherland with five souls over fifteen years of age was to be acknowledged a master or colonist, and entitled to claim 100 Morgen (200 acres) of land. When the settlements of these masters increased so as to become villages, towns, or cities, the company was bound to confer upon them subaltern or municipal governments.[2]

---

of the manor was injurious to the growth of liberal ideas. The manor was a self-governing community." Is it not true, however, that it was "a self-governing community," only in so far as the power of the lord of the manor had been restricted by the people? And would not the "liberal ideas" of the Dutch settlers have borne earlier and richer fruit if the character of the manor had not checked their growth? This is evidently the opinion of Mr. Fernow who (in his introduction to vol. XIII. of Docs. relating to Col. Hist. of N. Y.), says that the "object of the Patroons had been, at first when they obtained their privileges in 1629, rather a participation in the Indian trade than the colonization of the country ; their new plan was to divide the province into manors for a privileged class to the exclusion of the hardy and industrious pioneer and sturdy and independent yeoman." All the more noteworthy and commendable, is the persistent and successful struggle of the "sturdy and independent yeoman" of Holland in fighting his way towards free representative government when opposed by such extensive manorial grants to the Patroons, who were in favor with the powerful West India Company.

[1] Docs. Relating to Col. Hist. of N. Y., I., pp. 119–123.

[2] The charter of 1640, which thus contained more liberal provisions for agricultural settlement, still retained clauses for erecting manors under Patroons ; but they could only claim about a quarter of the territory which they might have claimed under previous charters, and their authority over the colonists was somewhat lessened. In 1655, the Directors of the West India Company reiterated their disinclination, any longer to grant colonies like Rensselaerswyck to Patroons. Docs. Relating to Col. Hist. of N. Y., XIV., pp. 332–3.

The Dutch settlers, at this time established in New Amsterdam and vicinity, had given Kieft, the Director-General, to understand plainly that they demanded a voice in the government. In 1641, the brutal murder of Claes Smits by an Indian was the occasion of the first recognition by the Director-General of the people's demand. "All the masters and heads of families, residents of New Amsterdam, and its neighborhood, were therefore, invited to assemble in the fort on the 28th day of August then and there to determine on 'something of the first importance.'"[1] This, the first popular assembly in New Netherland, promptly chose "Twelve Select Men"[2]—all emigrants from Holland—to consider the propositions submitted by the Director.[3]

The step towards freedom gained at this time was never lost. Before Kieft dismissed them,[4] as having served in settling the Indian affair, the purpose for which they were elected, the "Twelve Men" had demanded for New Amsterdam, and the neighboring settlements, the popular representation of Holland, urging that "the Council of a small village in Fatherland consists of five @. seven Schepens."[5] In 1643,

---

[1] O'Callaghan, Hist. of New Netherland, I., p. 241.

[2] Mr. Palfrey would apparently have us believe that this selection of representatives by the Dutch settlers at New Amsterdam must somehow be accounted for by a borrowing of the methods of the Dorchester colonists in Massachusetts (see p. 10, *supra*). Neither perhaps had need to borrow what had been known for centuries to the ancestors of both, but certainly the Dutch knew, even better than the English, the advantages of representative government.

[3] Brodhead's Hist. of N. Y., p. 317.

[4] Hol., Doc. III., pp. 175-180, cited by O'Callaghan, Hist. N. N., Vol. I., pp. 248-9. The Director evidently did not intend that the "Twelve Men" should have any permanent share in the government. Whether he allowed them to be chosen merely "to serve him as a cloak, and as cats-paws,"—perhaps to shield him from responsibility, as Van der Donck strenuously asserts, or whether for some more worthy purpose, the fact remains that it was a concession by the arbitrary ruler in the direction of representative government.

[5] Docs. Relating to Col. Hist. of N. Y., I., p. 202.

"Eight Men" were chosen by the commonalty and addressed the West India Company upon the serious Indian troubles. They renewed, in vigorous language,[1] the demand of the "Twelve Men" for representative government, and in 1646 the inhabitants of the village of "Breuckelen" (Brooklyn) were given the municipal privileges they desired. "They were to have the right of electing two schepens or magistrates, with full judicial powers, as in the Fatherland. Those who opposed the magistrates in the discharge of their duties were to be deprived of all share in the common lands adjoining the village."[2]  Thus at the first conferring of self-government upon this Dutch village, named for an ancient village in Utrecht, the evidence of a system of common land tenure is met with.

Under Stuyvesant, as under Kieft, the people of New Amsterdam clamored for their rights. Reforms were pressed upon him. New Amsterdam was in bad condition. Most of the lots were unimproved. Hog-pens, "little houses," and other nuisances encroached upon the public streets, and, in 1647, "fence viewers" were appointed, by whom, in addition to other duties, every new building had to be approved. In the same year, Stuyvesant and his council granted to the inhabitants of the Island of Manhattan and two or three adjacent towns, the privilege of nominating "a double number

---

[1] Docs. Relating to Col. Hist. of N. Y., I., p. 213. "It is impossible," they say in their letter to the Directors, "ever to settle this country until a different system be introduced here," and they suggest the election of representatives by the people to vote as deputies with the Director and Council.

[2] Brodhead, Hist. of N. Y., pp. 421–2. It is curious to note the strength, at that early day, of the opinion that "public office is a public trust." At New Amsterdam, in April, 1654, the Director-General sends following order to one Jan Everson Boot, who had been elected schepen of "Breuckelen." "If you will not accept to serve as schepen for the welfare of the village of Breuckelen with others, your fellow residents, then you must prepare yourself to sail in the ship 'King Solomon' for Holland, agreeably to your own utterance," he having said he would rather go than serve. Docs. Relating to Col. Hist. of N. Y., XIV., p. 255.

of persons from the most notable, reasonable, honest and respectable of our subjects, from whom we might select a single number of Nine Men to them best known, to confer with us and our council, as their Tribunes, on all means to promote the welfare of the commonalty as well as that of the country." [1]

Not, however, until 1652 did the people succeed in obtaining for New Amsterdam itself a municipal form of government. In accordance with the 17th clause of the Provisional Order of 1650,[2] it consisted of " one schout, two burgomasters [3] and five schepens,[4] to be elected by the citizens in the manner usual in ' this city of Amsterdam,' to act as a Court of Justice with the right of appeal in certain cases ' to the Supreme Court of Judicature.' " This advance towards a representative government in New Amsterdam marked the beginning of a new era throughout the whole of New Netherland, which was not, however, without its struggles between the people and Stuyvesant's arbitrary exercise of power.[5] In

---

[1] O'Callaghan, Hist. of New Netherland, II., p. 39.—(Citing Alb. Rec. VII., pp. 72-74, 81-84.)

These " Nine Men " were of more importance in the affairs of the colony than any previous representative body.—Brodhead's Hist. of N. Y., p. 474.

[2] O'Callaghan, Hist. of New Netherland, II., p. 192.—(Citing Alb. Rec. IV., pp. 68, 72, 73, 75; VIII., pp. 8-13, 16-19, 42.)

[3] The name and office of the burgomaster in Holland may be traced as early as the 14th century.—O'Callaghan, Hist. of New Netherland, II., p. 211.

[4] The word schepen, meaning, as here, one of the local magistrates in Holland, is older still, probably originating about 1270, says one writer; but that date is not early enough. The word was used in an instrument said to have been signed and sealed in 1217, and quoted by Motley, The Dutch Republic, I., p. 35.

[5] The difficulties with which the people had to contend are given a ludicrous coloring in a letter from Van Dinclagen to Van der Donck: " To describe the state of this government to one well acquainted with it is a work of supererogation; it is washing a black-a-moor white. Our Grand Muscovy Duke goes on as usual, resembling somewhat the wolf—the older he gets the worse he bites. He proceeds no longer by words or letters but by arrests and stripes."—O'Callaghan, Hist. of New Netherland, II., p. 170; citing Hol. Doc. VI., pp. 5, 7, 53-60, 67, 68. The letter was in Latin.

April, 1652, Beverwyck was declared to be independent of the Patroon's colony, "and the germ of the present city of Albany was released from feudal jurisdiction,"[1] its court being established at Fort Orange. Two years later, Breuckelen and adjacent towns[2] secured the privilege from Stuyvesant of having a greater number of schepens, and district courts were organized, (composed of delegates from each town-court, together with the schout,) which had general authority over roads, the establishment of churches and schools, and the making of local laws, subject to the approval of the provincial government.[3]

About the same time, there came an increase in immigration, both from abroad and from New England. English settlers, fleeing from the persecutions of New England, had already established themselves in towns under the Dutch government, which, in New Netherland, still allowed the broad religious toleration of Holland. With the exception of some persecution of the quakers under Stuyvesant's personal lead, the principles which made Holland the asylum of the persecuted were observed by the Dutch in America. There came to the Hudson river, Walloons from the Spanish Netherlands, Huguenots from France, Puritans from New England, and Waldenses from Piedmont,—all seeking freedom from persecution, and finding it in New Netherland rather than in New England, where, at this time in Massachusetts colony, civil rights were dependent upon church membership. In New Netherland, such rights, fought for step by step, depended simply upon the ownership in land, as did the rights of the members of the early Germanic village community.

Turning from this hasty sketch of the growth of representative government in New Amsterdam and vicinity before the year 1650, we may take this middle year of the 17th

[1] Brodhead's Hist. of N. Y., p. 535.
[2] Midwout and Amersfoort.
[3] Brodhead's Hist. of N. Y., p. 580.

century as an approximate starting point for an exami-
ination in detail of the peculiar characteristics of the
Dutch village communities; for, from this time forward, the
agricultural settlements increased more rapidly, and, under
conditions of freer government, villages and towns grew
up, on lands granted directly to those who were to cultivate the soil. Hoping to advance such settlement, van Tien-
hoven, the Dutch Secretary under Stuyvesant, sent information
to Holland in March, 1650, in regard to taking up land in
New Netherland. " Before beginning to build," he said,
" 'twill above all things be necessary to select a well located
spot on some river or bay, suitable for the settlement of a
village or hamlet. This is previously properly surveyed and
divided into lots, with good streets, according to the situation
of the place. This hamlet can be fenced all around with high
palisades or long boards and closed with gates.[1] . . . Outside the village or hamlet, other land must be laid out which
can in general be fenced and prepared at the most trifling
expense."[2]

The draft of " Freedoms and Exemptions," in the same year,
(1650) states that, " on the arrival of the aforesaid persons in
New Netherland they shall be allowed and granted the privilege of choosing and taking up under quit rent or as a fief,
such parcels of land as they shall in any way be able to cultivate for the production of all sorts of fruits and crops of
those parts," on condition that they should be deprived of the
land, if it were not cultivated within a year. They were to
" enjoy exemption from Tenths," for a term of — years, " and

---

[1] This enclosure is clearly analogous to the *Hedge* of the early Teutonic
village, which, through the Saxon Tun, is perpetuated in our English word,
Town. For the existence of a similar survival in New England and a more
complete statement of the interesting derivation of the word Town, see
" Studies," I., " Germanic Origin of New England Towns," pp. 26–31.

[2] Docs. Relating to Col. Hist. of N. Y., I., pp. 365, 367–8. This may be
called the Village Mark in New Netherland,—a larger *town* around the
smaller.

thenceforth one additional year's exemption for every legitimate child they shall convey thither or get there." They might also cut and draw timber from the public forests, and hunt and fish in the public woods and streams.[1] The company sometimes advanced land, farm implements, and cattle, for the term of six years, the farmer being "bound to pay yearly one hundred guilders and eighty pounds of butter rent for the cleared land and bouwerie."[2]

It has been noted[3] that as early as 1646, the village of Breuckelen had about it common lands in which the inhabitants had a share, to be taken as a penalty from those who opposed the schepens, or magistrates, of the town. In New Amsterdam itself, where the people had not at first settled for agricultural purposes, the right of pasturage in common lands prevailed. In 1649, the Director and Council passed a resolution to the effect that "the farmers on the Island Manhattan requesting by petition a free pasturage on the Island Manhattan, between the plantation[4] of Schepmoes and the fence of the Great Bouwery, No. 1, the petitioners' request is provisionally granted, and that no new plantation shall be made or granted between said fencing."[5] What is now City Hall

---

[1] Docs. Relating to Col. Hist. of N. Y., I., p. 401.

[2] Docs. Relating to Col. Hist. of N. Y., I., p. 371. This word "bouwerie," which occurs so frequently in early Dutch documents, is an interesting one. The verb in Dutch is "bouwen," to build; to till, plough. "Bouwerie" is used to designate in most cases, not only the portion of the land which is tilled or ploughed, but also that portion on which the farm *buildings* stand. In other words, it means usually the "home-lot," which, in the village communities on the Hudson, as in those on the Rhine, and in other parts of Europe (Laveleye, Prim. Prop., p. 112), was in early times the only holding that was strictly in severalty.

[3] See p. 20, *supra*.

[4] Here, as often, "plantation" and "Bouwery" are used as opposite terms. Dr. O'Callaghan, Hist. of New Netherland, II., p. 291, Note, says of this use: "By bouweries are meant those farms on which the family resided; by plantations those which were partly cultivated, but on which no settlers dwelt."

[5] Docs. Relating to Col. Hist. of N. Y., XIV., p. 110.

Park in New York, bounded by Broadway, Nassau, Ann and Chambers streets, was, as late as 1686, perhaps much later, known as the Village Commons, where the droves of cattle were sent morning and evening to pasture.[1]

These village rights of common in regard to land were accompanied, in New Amsterdam, by rights of common participation in the deliberative assembly of the people, as they were in the forests of Germany centuries before. The record runs: "Tuesday Novbr. 11. 1653. Present at the meeting in the City Hall of New Amsterdam," two Burgomasters and three Schepens named. Then follows the statement that "some of the most influential burghers and inhabitants of this city having been lawfully summoned the following appeared," naming twenty-three. "To whom the said Hon[bl] Burgomasters and Schepens propose that, whereas they have asked the community to provide means for paying the public expenses and keeping in repair the works . . . the aforesaid Magistrates ask the Community whether they will submit to such ordinances and taxes, as the Magistrates may consider proper and necessary for the government of this city. They all answered 'Yes!' and promised to obey the Hon[bl] Magistrates in every thing as good inhabitants are in duty bound to do confirming it with their signatures."[2] One needs no great power of the imagination to fancy that he hears, in the unanimously spoken "Yes" of the Dutch assembly, something very like the shaking of spears and clashing of shields[3] with which the sturdy, warlike Teutons signified assent to the plans of their chieftains in the open-air meetings of the tribe!

The voice of the colonial settlers had found tolerably free expression in local affairs, in some of the village communities[4] on Long Island, earlier than the organization of municipal

---

[1] Valentine, History of New York City, p. 281.

[2] Docs. Relating to the Col. Hist. of N. Y., XIV., p. 220.

[3] Green's Hist. of the English People, I., p. 15.

[4] "Gravesande" (1645); Breuckelen (1646); Amersfoort (1647).

government in New Amsterdam. The majority of the settlers in the neighboring hamlets were Dutch ; some, however,
were English, who had come from New England to enjoy
religious freedom among the Dutch colonists. They took
their lands by Dutch title, and willingly placed themselves
under Dutch laws and modes of government.[1]   Director
Kieft's patent[2] to the town of Gravesend, in the year 1645,
when a few settlers had moved there from New England, is a
veritable Dutch charter of civil and religious freedom.   The
patentees, it reads, were "to have and enjoye the free libertie
of conscience according to the costome and manner of Holland, without molestation or disturbance from any Madgis-
trate or Madgistrates or any other ecclesiasticall Minister that
may p'tend iurisdiction over them, with libertie likewise for
them the s$^d$ patentees theyr associates heyres &c. to erect a
bodye politique and ciuill combination amongst themselves, as
free men of this Province & of the Towne of Gravesend & to
make such ciuill ordinances as the Maior part of y$^e$ Inhabitants ffree of the Towne shall think fitting for theyr quiett
and peaceable subsisting & to nominate elect & choose
three of y$^e$ ablest approved honest men & them to present
annuallie to y$^e$ Gouernor Generall of this Province for the
tyme being, for him y$^e$ said Gouern$^r$ to establish and con-
firme;" which three men were to act as a local court with the
usual jurisdiction.   Five years after this patent was granted,
the record of "severall orders agreed vppon by and with consent and approbation of the inhabitants of Gravesend," shows
that "the first inhabitants agree togeather att Amesfort that
they would fence in a certaine quantitie of Land to Conteine
eight and twenty shares, the s$^d$ land to be fenced with post and
raile in one Common fence and to have it compleated by a
certaine daye by them agreed vppon; vppon the penaltie of for-
feiting as much as the rest of the s$^d$ fence might come vnto;

---

[1] Docs. Relating to Col. Hist. of N. Y., I., p. 181.
[2] Doc. Hist. of N. Y., I., p. 411.   (See Gravesend Records).

. . . . The said eight and twenty shares were devided by lott; and every one injoyned to build and inhabit in the towne by a daye agreed vppon for the mutual strengthening of one another, for the peace with the Indians being new, and rawe there was still feares of theyre vprising to warre. . . . It was likewise agreed & ordered that none of the inhabitants should sell theyre lotts to any whatsoeuer, but first to propound it to the towne in generall[1] & in case the towne would not buye then hee to have libertie to sell to any, vnlesse hee were notoriouslie detected for an infamous person or a disturber of the common peace . . . It was therefore ordered that the men should at several times as they thought fitting view all the fences and when they found defects to giue warning to the neighbors to make upp theyre fences according to order."[2]

The extent to which the principles of holding property in common prevailed among the Dutch settlers in the vicinity of New Amsterdam, with reference to personal property as well as to land, is evidenced by a deed[3] for land and *cattle* on Long Island in 1651, granting, "all whatsoever the vendor has thereon and is belonging to him together with thirty-five and one half (*sic*) goats;" but the deed adds : "which the purchaser now takes at his risk and hazard ,"—a saving clause perhaps to avoid trouble in the division of the odd goat!

A document dated August 27, 1657,[4] indicates the custom of furnishing to a town a certain quantity of meadow land, presumably beyond the town proper. It states that Petrus Stuyvesant on petition showing the need of the inhabitants of "the new begun Town of Utrecht and of those who might

---

[1] This was certainly a serious encumbrance upon individual rights in land. The same restriction is found in the Germanic Mark, where "no one could sell his property to a stranger without the consent of his associates, who always had a right of preemption."—Laveleye, Prim. Prop., p. 118.

[2] Docs. Relating to Col. Hist. of N. Y., XIV., pp. 128-9.

[3] Docs. Relating to Col. Hist. of N. Y., XIV., p. 143.

[4] Doc. History of N. Y., I., p. 416.

hereafter dwell there, allowed unto them as to others a parcel
of meadow land lying on Long Island by the easterly Hook
of the Bay of the North River, over against Conyen Island."
Two years afterward, it is recorded that twenty-four inhabitants having plantations drew lots by numbers for the
meadows which had been divided into twenty-four parcels.
Two plantations, whose owners were named, might draw two
lots each.[1] This distinction between meadow or pasture land
and the tilled land, is observed also in the documents relating
to the proposed establishment in 1658 of "a new village at the
north-eastern extremity of Manhattan Island, ' for the pro-
motion of agriculture, and as a place of amusement for the
citizens of New Amsterdam.' To encourage this settlement
to which the name of ' New Haerlem ' was given, each inhabitant was to receive from eighteen to twenty-four morgens of
tillage, and from six to eight morgens of pasture land . . .
The magistrates were to be nominated at first by the settlers,
. . . "[2] Another illustration of the marked separation of
lands that were to be devoted to different uses, is found in the
provision for a "Towneshipp" on Staten Island : "A Towne,
the which shall bee divided into lotts according to the number
of Inhabitants proposed . . . That each home lott shall
have . . . acres of Ground to build a house upon and for
gardens or other necessary accomodacons. . . . That there
shall bee allotted of Ploughland or Arable ground . . . acres
and of Meadow a convenient proporcon." Liberty of conscience, and the selection of their own minister, was granted.
The latter was to have a "lott of ground proporconable with
the Rest," to be held for succeeding ministers.[3]

---

[1] Doc. Hist. of N. Y., I., p. 416.

[2] O'Callaghan, Hist. of New Netherland, II., p. 428.—(Citing Alb. Rec.
VII , pp. 420–22; XXIV., pp. 368-9).

[3] Docs. Relating to Col. Hist. of N. Y., XIII., p. 425.

Bearing upon this division of the land in the early settlements about New
Amsterdam, a passage may here be cited not merely as a study in land
tenure, but also as a study in English. It relates to the present town of

In the cluster of Dutch village communities at the mouth of the Hudson, many of the peculiar customs of Holland also prevailed, which were not specially connected with land-holding. An order with regard to "waggon racing," provides that "No person shall race with carts and wagons, in the streets within the villages, but the driver while passing through villages must walk by the side of his horse or vehicle,[1] according to the edict of the 12th of July, 1657." An edict of "the 15th Dec^r 1657," relating to inn-keepers, is what might be called an early Civil Damage act: "All tavern keepers to be held · liable for willingly permitting fighting or wounding in their houses, and when such breaches of the peace take place, they shall inform the officer of the same, on the penalty of having their trade stopped."[2]

---

Jamaica, which then had the no doubt appropriate Dutch name of "Rustdorp" (quiet-village), and it purports to be "a true coppy taken out of y^e town-booke by Daniel Denton, Clark, y^e 29th off August, 1661." It goes on to say: "It is farther voted & agreed upon by the town y^t as y^o medows are devided by lot above specified so they shall continue ffor perpetuity without any ffurther devision till y^e bee Layed out in particular & y^n every man to take his share in y^e neck where the now, & as y^e town do enlarge w^th inhabitants y^o shall bee devided proportionably to every neck till y^e bee layd out." Docs. Relating to Col. Hist. of N. Y., XIV., p. 506.

[1] The writer has somewhere seen it stated that this custom of walking by the side of horse or vehicle is still observed in some villages of the more northern provinces of Holland.

[2] Doc. Hist. of N. Y., I., p. 424.

It might be considered an unpardonable omission, for one who was referring to the peculiar customs of early New York, not to mention some of the causes which were considered directly responsible for bringing on a certain "warr with the Indians." Among the reasons given, are these: "For men wearing long hair and perriwigs made of women's hair.

"For women wearing borders of hair and for cutting curling and laying out their hair and disguising themselves by following strange fashions in their apparel.

"For prophaneness in the people in not frequenting their meetings, and others going away before the blessing is pronounced."

Docs. Relating to Col. Hist. of N. Y., III., p. 243. (Date [probably 1614–92], and authenticity not vouched for).

A hundred miles north of New Amsterdam, the first
Dutch adventurers had erected, in 1614, on the western bank
of the Hudson river, a small block house called the " Ron-
duit." [1] The land about it remained unsettled till the year
1652 or 3, when a few persons who had been members of the
colony of Rensselaerswyck, desiring to escape the feudal
restrictions of the manor, settled upon the Indian tract called
Atkarkarton, in the region known as the Esopus. [2] In 1661,
this Dutch settlement had grown to an extent which induced
the inhabitants to desire separation from Fort Orange, of
which it had hitherto been an appendage, so as to obtain a
local court of justice and a settled ministry.

Stuyvesant " accordingly conferred a charter on the Esopus,
to which place, in commemoration of the fact that the soil was a
free gift from the Indians, he gave the name of ' Wiltwyck.' " [3]
The charter granted to this village indicates very well the
scope of the powers possessed by incorporated towns in New
Netherland at that time. It provided that " the aforesaid
Director-General and Council, considering the increased population of said village, resolve to favor its inhabitants with a
subaltern court of justice, and to organize it as far as possible,
and the situation of the country will permit, in conformity
with the customs of the city of Amsterdam in Holland, but
so, that from all judgments an appeal may be made to the
Director-General and Council in New Netherland, who shall
reserve the power to give their final decision ; " that the court
of justice " shall consist of a sheriff, [4] being *in loco*, who shall

---

[1] It is now Rondout, recently incorporated with the city of Kingston. It
was the Dutch word meaning a "small fort." In Docs. Relating to Col.
Hist. of N. Y., XIII., p. 149, it is called "Redout ;" at p. 257, it is called
" Redoubt."

[2] O'Callaghan, Hist. of New Netherland, II., pp. 356-7 ; also Brodhead's
Hist. of N. Y., p. 536. Esopus creek still retains the name then applied also
to the region through which it ran.

[3] O'Callaghan, Hist. of New Netherland, II., p. 432. (Citing Alb. Rec.
XIX., pp. 36, 112, 114, 137-140).

[4] Roeloff Swartwout was soon after appointed the first sheriff at Wiltwyck.
Among his instructions is the following : " He shall take rank of the Burgo-

summon in the name of the Director-General and Council, the appointed schepens, and preside at their meeting ; and with him three schepens, who for the present time and ensuing year, . . . are elected by the Director-general and Council aforesaid." This court was to give final judgment in civil suits involving fifty guilders, or less, in amount; in other cases an appeal lay to the Director-General and Council. In criminal cases the local court had power to arrest, imprison, and transfer the delinquent to the Director-General, but not to act further except in regard to the lesser crimes, and in all such cases an appeal lay to the supreme authority. One clause of the charter reads : "All inhabitants of the Esopus are, till further orders, either from the Lords Patroons, or their higher magistrates, subjected and may be summoned before the aforesaid Sheriff and Commissaries, who shall hold their court, in the village aforesaid, every fortnight—harvest time excepted—unless necessity or occasion might otherwise require." [1] Subject to certain requirements of approval from the Director-General and Council, they might act in regard to public roads, the enclosure of lands, the building of churches and schools, etc. In conclusion the charter provides that "whereas, it is customary in our Fatherland and other well regulated governments, that annually some change takes place in the magistracy, so that some new ones are appointed, and some are continued to inform the newly appointed, so shall the Schepens, now confirmed, pay due attention to the conversation,.conduct and abilities of honest and decent persons, inhabitants of their respective villages, to inform the Director-General and Council, about the time of the next election, as to who might be sufficiently qualified to be then elected by the Director-General and Council."

---

masters and Schepens and sit in their meeting, also to exhort the culprits, sentenced by the Court, before sentence is passed on behalf of the magistrates." Docs. Relating to Col. Hist. of N. Y., XIII., p. 158.

[1] O'Callaghan, Hist. of New Netherland, II., pp. 436-7.

Even before the incorporation of this village, there were
evidences in the grants of land at Esopus of the distinction
between the bouweries, or "home lots,"[1] meadow land, and
.wood land.   In a patent dated September, 1656, by Stuyvesant and his council to one Cristoffel Davids, he was granted
thirty-six morgens of land, "with as much hayland (meadow)
as shall *pro rata* be allowed to the other bouweries."[2]   About
the same time there was a patent to Johanna de Laet, of land
"containing altogether in arable lands, meadows and wood
land five hundred morgens."[3]   After the establishment of the
local court of justice, one of the first cases which came before
the three schepens, shows very well the existence of the custom
of common pasturage.   One Blanshan complained that the
herdsman did not "bring his cows home in time, that he had
not brought them in two days." . The herdsman answered :
"If they don't bring their cattle by the drove I can't care for
them."   This was the view of the court.[4]

Only two years after Wiltwyck received its charter, came
the massacre by the Indians, June 7, 1663.   The savages,
entering.the palisaded village just before noon while the farmers were in the fields, killed many of the defenceless women
and children, took some forty-five others into captivity, and
burned a part of the town.   Seventy inhabitants were missing
when the Indians were finally routed by the assembled villagers.   This seemed to be the beginning of the misfortunes
which immediately preceded the surrender of the Dutch to the
English in September of the following year.   The situation
became alarming ; "an expensive war was being waged against
the Indians ; the Company's territory was invaded by Con-
necticut ; the English villages were in a state of revolt, and
the public treasury was exhausted."[5]   In this extremity, the

[1] See page 24, *supra.*
[2] Docs. Relating to Col. Hist. of N. Y., XIII., pp. 69-70.
[3] Docs. Relating to Col. Hist. of N. Y., XIII., pp. 71-72.
[4] Researches of the late Jonathan W. Hasbrouck.
[5] O'Callaghan, Hist. of New Netherland, II., p. 490.

burgomasters and schepens at New Amsterdam requested the Director and Council to call a meeting of delegates from the several towns, " to take into consideration the state of the province." " It was at this gloomy juncture," says Dr. O'Callaghan, " when it became evident that the country was held only on sufferance, and authority felt itself utterly powerless that the principle of popular REPRESENTATION was, for the first time, fully recognized in this province."[1] Two deputies were elected by plurality votes of the inhabitants at New Amsterdam, Rensselaerswyck, Fort Orange, Wiltwyck, New Haerlem, Staten Island, Breukelen, Midwout, Amersfoort, New Utrecht, Boswyck, and Bergen.

Even such a popular assembly as this, was not able to resist the tide of events which, in September of 1664, swept New Netherland from the hands of the Dutch and placed it under English rule. The Dutch colonists themselves did not seem averse to a change in government. They were doubtless wearied by their long struggle for the popular rights enjoyed in their Fatherland, and hoped that they might gain additional freedom under England's rule. In that, they were doomed to disappointment; it took nearly twenty years under English supremacy for them to reach the same point—the election of a popular general representative assembly [2]—which they had just gained from the Dutch government before its surrender to Colonel Nicolls.

The Dutch of New Amsterdam vigorously contended, at this time, for their rights, and thus the articles of capitulation, which Nicolls consented to in the "Governor's Bowery,"[3] contained many liberal clauses. They provided, among other

---

[1] O'Callaghan, Hist. of New Netherland, II., p. 505.

[2] This was the general assembly of 1683, which divided the Hudson river valley into counties (see Docs. Relating to Col. Hist. of N. Y., XIII., p. 575), and was the beginning of regular representative government for the whole province of New York.

[3] What is now the Bowery in New York City was doubtless originally so called from Gov. Stuyvesant's "home-lot" and its buildings.

things, that "all people shall continue free denizens, and shall enjoy their, lands, houses, goods, shipps, wheresoever they are within this country, and dispose of them as they please;" that they "shall enjoy their own customs concerning their inheritances," and "the liberty of their consciences in Divine Worship and church discipline."[1] As a whole, the immediate changes which the surrender wrought in the government were nominal rather than substantive. It had been agreed that in the inferior offices there should be no changes until the next regular election, and although New Amsterdam became New York, the same city government of schout, burgomasters, and schepens went on for nearly a year. On the 12th of June, 1665, there was published what the record[2] calls: "The Governor Revocation of y⁰ fforme of Government of New Yorke under y⁰ style of Burgomast[r] & Schepens" It declares: "That by a particular commission such persons shall be authorized to putt the Lawes in execucon in whose abilityes prudence & good affection to his Ma^ties service and y⁰ Peace and happinesse of this Governm^t I have especial reason to put confidence, which persons so constituted and appointed shall be knowne and called by the Name & Style of Mayor or Aldermen and Sheriffe, according to the custome of England in other his Ma^ties Corporacons." Eight years later (1673) Benckes and Evertsen's charter[3] reinstated the Dutch government for six months before the English again took possession of the territory.

The Duke of York's Laws[4] published and given to Colonel Nicolls, the Deputy Governor, in 1664, but not introduced till Sept. 22, 1676, recognize, with some changes of phrase-

---

[1] Docs. Relating to Col. Hist. of N. Y., II., pp. 250, 251.

[2] Doc. Hist. of N. Y., I., p. 389.

[3] For many of the papers of this period see Docs. Relating to Col. Hist. of N. Y., II., pp. 571–731.

[4] These laws may be conveniently referred to, as published under direction of the Secretary of the Commonwealth of Pennsylvania in 1879, with interesting historical matter relating to that State.

ology, the existence of many of the village customs which prevailed in the earlier Dutch settlements. Constables were to be chosen yearly, " by the plurality of the votes of the freeholders in each town." The " overseers shall be eight in Number, men of good fame and life, Chosen by the plurality of voyces of the freeholders in each Town." Thus the voters of the villages were, as before, the freeholders ; the suffrage continued to be based upon land. Similar methods of holding the land in common still obtained, and were recognized in the Duke's Laws. " Every person interested in the improvement of Common fields inclosed for Corn or other Necessary use shall from time to time, make and keep his part of the fence Sufficiently Strong and in constant repair, to secure the Corn and other fruits therein, and shall not put, cause, or permit any Cattle to be put in so long as any Corn or other fruits shall be growing or remain upon any part of the Land so Enclosed." Fence-viewers, such as had earlier been appointed in New Amsterdam and other Dutch towns, were also provided for in the English laws just quoted, " for all or each Common field belonging to the Town where they dwell ; to view the Common fences within their trust." Further, " all cattle and hoggs shall be markt with the publique mark of the Town to which they belong and the private mark of the owner, and whatsoever Swine or greater Cattle, horses excepted shall be found in the woods or Commons unmarked are Lyable to poundage." [2] The character of the courts proposed by

---

[1] It is interesting to note that in the Duke's Laws, the rules laid down for the building of line fences show a marked distinction between the " home-lots " and all other land. Between the " home-lots," the line fence must be made and maintained by both owners, even if only one wished to " improve " by fencing. Of other lands, only such as " improved " the land paid for the fencing. He " shall Compell no man to make any fence with him except he also Improve in Several." ·

[2] The village pound is so old an institution ("older than the King's Bench," says Sir Henry Maine, in Early History of Institutions, p. 263), that the survival is a matter of special interest. Dr. H. B. Adams has called attention to its early existence at Hatfield, and has noted its deriva-

these laws was similar to that of the earlier Dutch tribunals. The Court of Sessions[1] held within the "Riding," by the constable and justices of the peace, took the place essentially of that of the schout and schepens under the Dutch. The Court of Assizes, held once a year at New York, was a higher Court, and the local Town Courts were lower than the Court of Sessions, and were constituted by the constable with at least five overseers sitting in judgment upon matters belonging peculiarly to the town.

Governor Nicolls five years after the first English possession, in answer "to the Severall Queries Relating to the Planters in the Territories of his R. H. S. the Duke of Yorke · in America,"[2] reports : " 1st. The Governour and Council with the High Sheriffe and the Justices of the Peace in the Court of the Generall assizes have the Supreme Power of making altering and abolishing any Laws in this Government . . . 2nd. The Land is naturally apt to produce Corne & Cattle so that the severall proportions or dividents of Land are alwaies allowed with respect to the numbers of the Planters, what they are able to manage and in w[t] time to accomplish their undertaking, the feed of Cattell is free in Commonage tʰ all Townships. The Lots of Meadow or Corne

tion from the Saxon *pyndan*, to pen or enclose.—(Studies, First Series. New England Towns, p. 32). In the record of the transactions in the town of Wiltwyck, 1667, may be found the following instructions for the "poundmaster (or Encloser)." " No horses or Cattle must run on the lands before the first of September. And if anything but working horses and calves are found on any ones land, or his neighbors, he shall bring it to the pound yard and the owner must pay full pound money," etc.

[1] At Wiltwyck, "a Court of Sessions convened April 26, (probably in 1675), composed of Captain Chambers, justice of the peace, George Hall, sheriff, Cornelius B. Slecht, W. Nottingham, Jan Eltinge and Jan Brigs." —(History of J. W. Hasbrouck, p. 176). At the same time "a record was . . . made of a jury, viz: William Ashfordby, Wessel Ten Broeck, Lowies Duboys, Mattys Mattysen, Jacob Adriaense, D. J. Schmoes, Jacobus Elmendorf." Mr. Hasbrouck considers this to be probably the first jury in America. Assault and battery the chief offence.

[2] Doc. Hist. of N. Y., I., p. 59.

Ground are peculiar to each Planter." Yet it should be noted
that these " Lots of Meadow or Corne Ground," which are
spoken of as "peculiar to each Planter," were probably not
separately fenced as individual holdings until some years
afterward. At the Esopus, and probably elsewhere along
the river, it was the custom of the villagers to enclose many lots
or farms outside of the stockade, in one enclosure ; each owner
of the land enclosed, building in proportion to his valuation,
a part of what was called the " Ring-fence,"[1] which it was the
fence-viewer's duty to look after. In the Kingston Records,[2] at the county clerk's office, a grant dated August 25,
1701, conveys land "running . . . about south west unto
the Ring-fence, and from the said Ring-fence north west
in the woods." In 1676 an order to the magistrates of
Esopus, speaks of the "inconvenience, prejudice and great
charge to all the Inhabitants of these parts, to maintaine an
Extraordinary ffence many Miles Long,"[3] and bids the farmers
to move their houses within the town. Just when these
extensive common fences, enclosing many holdings of the
arable land, disappeared, is doubtful.[4] It was probably by a

---

[1] Researches of the late J. W. Hasbrouck.

[2] Liber AA. of Deeds, p. 265.

[3] Docs. Relating to Col. Hist. of N. Y., XIII., p. 495.

[4] The circular, or ring-fence, was the object of special enactment in the
early laws of New York. "An Act for regulating the Fences in the County
of Ulster. Passed the 18th of October, 1701," recites that " whereas in the
County of Ulster, the Inhabitants there are accustomed to make circular
Fences, for the surrounding of their Land which they manure, by which
Means great Quantities of Lands, are surrounded with the said circular
Fence; and those who are in the Middle of the said Lands, have their
Fields secured by the said Fence, yet have not contributed, nor will con-
tribute their Proportion of the charge of the said Fences: That the same
may be remedied for the future; I. BE IT ENACTED *by his Honour the Lieu-
tenant Governor, and Council, and Representatives, convened in General Assem-
bly, and by the Authority of the same,* That as to all Lands within the said
County of Ulster, which now are, or hereafter shall be surrounded with a
Circular Fence, the Owners or Possessors thereof shall, in proportion to the
Quantities of Land they have within the said Fence, pay and contribute to

gradual change; but it is certain that the rights of common
in pasture and woodland prevailed in the Hudson river towns
a long time after the cultivated lands had become separately
enclosed by the individual holders. At Kingston in 1792,—
a hundred years later than the period we have been examining, in a lease now in the archives of the Ulster Historical
Society,—Johannes J. Jansen describes one of his lots of
"orchard and meadow land," as "lying west and adjoining
the Lands of Jacob Ten Brouck and the Plains or Common."
"House-lot" and "Armebouwery" are terms still in use at
that date, and even in the present century. [1]

Commonage of pasture and woodland appears in communities established much later than those we have hitherto been
examining. The records in the County Clerk's office at
Goshen, although they do not begin until about 1700, show
that rights of common existed in Orange County for the next
hundred years at least. In 1686 Gov. Dongan gave a patent
to sixteen Dutch patentees to make what was to be called the
town of Orange, to be held of King James II., "in ffree &
Common Soccage according to the tenure of East Greenwich in
the county of Kent." [2] The record contains grants of lots in
this patent, with certain "privileges in the common or undivided land." [3] The Waywayanda and Tappan patents comprised large tracts of land granted to similar numbers of

the making of the said Fence;" then follows the conferring, upon any
Justice of the Peace in the county, of power, in case of non-payment, to assess
the proportion and direct the constable to levy on goods to the amount. A
similar act with regard to these circular fences passed in 1750. This act of
1750 speaks of "lands or Meadows, which they Use in Common among
them, in Tillage, Pasturage or Mowing," and the act of 1701 treats of the
fences surrounding "*Land which they manure.*" These designations show
that most of the holdings of the arable land were not separated by fences.

[1] See list of lots, as late as 1814, in the archives of the Ulster Historical
Society. "*Armebouwery*" probably meant an inferior home-lot, or poor
piece of tillable land.

[2] Orange County Records, Lib. B., p. 90.

[3] Orange County Records, Lib. B., p. 97.

proprietors and held largely in common. In "a release of survivorship by Joynt Tenantcy made between the Patentees of Waywayanda and entered at the request of said Patentees the 23rd day of September . . . 1706," each releases for himself, his heirs and assigns: "all their right of survivorship by Joynt Tennancy of in and to said full equall and undivided twelfth part of the before recited tracts of land."[1] Nearly ninety years later (Sept. 10, 1793), is recorded a grant "of four equal undivided thirty six parts of the said Lot piece or parcel of Land,"[2] of the Waywayanda patent. In a grant of 1720 was conveyed "all that certain Tract of Land situated in the Town Spott of Goshen in Orange County within the Colony of New York aforesaide containing eighty acres and known by number foore being one of the Home Lots."[3] In 1713 is recorded a grant of a lot of land "No. Two in the divided lands of Tapan . . . Together with an equall or proportionable right in the undivided land or commons of Tapan or Orange Towne agreeable and proportionable to what others shall have for the like quantitie of Morgens or acres,"[4]—which gives unmistakable evidence of the existence of the proportional rights of the villager in the general domain, known in England as "Common appendant," and found to exist in those village communities of the continent of Europe,[5] whence England's land customs came.

Not until near the beginning of the present century (1793), was any considerable portion of these common tracts divided

---

[1] Orange County Records, Lib. B., p. 3.
[2] Orange County Records, Lib. E., p. 277.
[3] Orange County Records, Lib. B. p. 277.
[4] Orange County Records, Lib. B., p. 81.
[5] "During the middle ages," says Laveleye, "the right to a share in the collective domain gradually ceased to be a personal right, and became a real right, a mere dependence on habitation. Only the owner of an entire farmstead (*Hube, Hoffstatt*) had a whole share in the *mark;* . . . The right of enjoyment in the fields, wood, meadow and water, was sold as an appendage of the *hube*." Laveleye, Prim. Prop., pp. 120–121.

by partition and allotment to individual proprietors, and it
was then done pursuant to acts of the Legislature of the
state.

In Dutchess County, which was settled a few years later
than Orange County, similar customs of land-holding prevailed for about the same length of time. The first deed
recorded in the Dutchess County Clerk's office at Poughkeepsie[1] is one dated Dec. 20, 1718, in which J. Jacobus Van
den Bogert granted to Capt. Barent Van Kleeck and others
a lot " For the proper and onley use benefitt and behoof of
the Inhabitance and Naborhod of pochkepsen aforesaid to
Bild and Maentaen a proper Mietenghous to worship the one
and onely . . . God according to the Ruels and Methodes as
it is agried and Concluded by the Sinod National kept at
Dordreght in the year 1618 and 1619 and that in the Neder
Dutch Lingo and manner as it is now used by the Clarsses
and Church of amsterdam with the benefitt of the Mieten-
hous yard for a Bureall place of Cristian Corps to the same
belonging." The community which thus, within fifteen
years after the first settlement, made such a permanent church
establishment, held their meadow and woodland, though
probably not their cultivated land, in common. The record
shows a grant, in 1707, by " Myndert harmse of pogkcepsink,

---

[1] The first mention of Poughkeepsie which I have found in the records
occurs in a quit-claim deed given by an Indian, reciting: " This fifth day
of May 1683 appeared before me, *Adrian Van Ilpendam*, Notary Public in
*New Albany* and the undersigned witnesses a *Highland* Indian called *Massany*,
who declares herewith that he has given as a free gift a bouwery to *Pieter
Lansingh* and bouwery to *Jan Smeedes* a young glazier also a waterfall near
the bank of the river to build a mill thereon. The waterfall is called
*Pooghkepesingh* and the land *Minnissingh* situate on the Eastside of the
river," etc. The witnesses were Cornelis van Dyk and Dirck Wesselsen.
This was undoubtedly the fall from which afterwards the Dutch gave the
name "Fall-kill" to the stream emptying into the Hudson at Poughkeepsie. A dye wood mill has for many years occupied the original site of
the mill of Jan Smeedes above mentioned.—Docs. Relating to Col. Hist. of
N. Y., XIII., p. 571.

. . . to Jan Osterom of Pogkeepsink " of a parcel of land
" with yᵉ previledge of cutting of timber and wood and Mowing of grasse for hay in yᵉ Meadows and pastering of Cattle
& horses in yᵉ woods of that part of yᵉ Land which now
belongeth to yᵉ heirs of yᵉ aforesaid Robert Sanders."[1] This
Robert Sanders here mentioned seems to have been the original patentee of a considerable tract of land from which grants
were made, always with the " common appendant " rights in
the unenclosed meadow and woodland. No town records of
this time remain to indicate the particular customs of pasturage about Poughkeepsie, but it is likely that in Dutchess,
as in Orange and Ulster Counties, the cattle were sent in droves
to the common pasture lands, each individual in the community designating his stock by a special brand or ear-mark.[2]

The first court house in Poughkeepsie was constructed of
wood furnished chiefly from "the commons." November 13,
1747, Jacobus Van den Bogert of Poughkeepsie precinct
gave to four justices of the peace a deed of lands for "Court
House & Goals," in which the grantor "for himself and
his heirs and assigns doth hereby Grant a privilege in his
Unimproved Lands or Commons for Cutting and Carrying
away all manner of wood and timber for Compleating and
Repairing the said Court House and Goals on the hereby
granted premises."[3] That the rights of commonage were
enjoyed generally by the neighborhood, appears in numerous
grants similar to the following : " Myndert harmse of pogkeepsink in Dutchess County . . . doe bargaine . . . unto the

---

[1] Dutchess County Records, Lib. A or 1, p. 7.

[2] The Register in the Orange County Clerk's office at Goshen, at page 32,
contains the following minute: " . . . 1704 The fourth Sessions. Ordered
That all the Inhabitants of this county doe the next Sessions Bring into the
Clark their markes of their Chatles &c, In order that they may be allowed
by the Court and entered by the said Clark in the publick Records. This
order publisht upon the County house door." The distinctive marks are
enumerated. Among others is found that of " Cornelius Herring for Horses
C H upon the nere buttock his neat Cattle sheep hogs &c. A hole in right
Eare and A Swallows Tale in the Left Eare."

[3] Dutchess County Records, Map 6.

said pieter u: ziele all that Certaine tract or parcell of Land scituate " and so on, " together w<sup>th</sup> the privilege of cutting grass for hay in y<sup>e</sup> Meadows as others of y<sup>e</sup> neighbours and ffree outdrift ffor horses and Cattle in y<sup>e</sup> woods.[1] This deed bears date, 1722/3, and reserves a yearly rent of "halfe a busshel of good winter wheat." In 1730, one Thomas Rathbone of Rhode Island granted to one John Gay and wife "and their heirs and assigns for ever one seventh part of all my Right or share of Land (both divided and undivided) in the Town of Pecapesy[2] in Dutchess County . . . together with the profits Priviledges and appurtenances unto the same belonging or in any wise appertaining."[3]

Less than one hundred years ago (Oct. 11, 1786), an affidavit was made by "johannis Swartwout and Samuel Curry, . . . that they are two of the owners and Proprietors of that certain tract undivided and parcel of Lands Tenements & heriditaments held in Common, situate . . . in the Precinct of Poughkeepsie . . . commonly called and known by the name of the Commons, and that they have given thirty days previous notice to the other owners and proprietors of the aforesaid tract of Lands . . . of their intention of applying to this Court [Common Pleas] for the appointment of Commissioners for the division of the same in pursuance of the act of the Legislature of the State of New York passed sixteenth of March, 1785 entitled ' an Act for the Partition of lands.' "[4] By means of such partition of the common lands, individual ownership of all property became universal in Dutchess, as it did in Orange County, just at the close of the last century.

There remain to be considered[5] two village communities, in some respects more marked in character, and more interest-

---

[1] Dutchess County Records, Lib. A. of Deeds, pp. 31-32.
[2] Poughkeepsie is said to have been spelled in more than forty different ways.
[3] Dutchess County Records, Lib. A. of Deeds, p. 103.
[4] Dutchess County Records, Map 13 and enclosed Docs.
[5] If the limits of this paper permitted, interesting facts of community-life might be gathered from other settlements on the Hudson. At Albany the

ing for purposes of study, than those already examined, because they combine with the customs of common land-holding, a local government and an exclusive family proprietorship peculiar to the earlier types of community-life among the Germanic peoples.

Just west of the town of Kingston, and adjoining it, lies the present town of Hurley, including land of which there were some grants to Dutch settlers who moved back from Wiltwyck as early as 1662. In distinction from the latter, and much older, place, the early settlers called it " Niew Dorp " (New Village).[1] The grants made by the Dutch government were confirmed after the English occupation, and in 1669, the same year in which Wiltwyck became Kingston, the " Niew Dorp " was named Hurley from the paternal estate of the English governor, Lovelace. There in Niew Dorp it was, that Louis Du Bois, the Walloon,[2] who afterwards became

---

records have been well preserved, but, so far as the writer has consulted them, they would yield nothing especially significant, aside from the facts already noted in other towns. From the earliest settlement until 1652, the inhabitants of Fort Orange, now Albany, were hampered by the feudal restrictions of the manor of Rensselaerswyck; at that time the separation took place and an independent court of justice was established at Fort Orange.

Interesting material also is afforded by the records relating to the settlements (one of them on the site of the present city of Newburgh) about the year 1710, made by Germans, who were known as the Palatines,—another instance of the close relationship between the Rhine and the Hudson, besides that afforded by New Paltz, as hereafter mentioned.

Doc. Hist. of New York, pp. 327–383, contains the papers relating to the Palatines, and at p. 347, in a document dated 1719, there is mentioned "A certain tract of land on the West side of Hudson's river above the high lands in the County of Ulster neer to a place called Quassaick containing two thousand one hundred and ninety acres laid out into nine lotts for the said Palatins and a glebe of five hundred acres for a Lutheran minister and his successors forever."

[1] Researches of J. W. Hasbrouck, referred to in Docs. Relating to Col. Hist. of N. Y., XIII, p. 412.

[2] The Walloons," says Dr. Baird (Huguenot Emigration to America, I., p. 149), " were the inhabitants of the region now comprised by the French départment du Nord, and the south western provinces of Belgium. They

the leader of the pioneer band that settled at New Paltz, had established himself, and from there the Indians took many captives in their retreat from the massacre at Wiltwyck in 1663, already mentioned. The Hurley (spelled Horly, hürly, and in several other ways) Commons is a term found in most of the early deeds of land in that vicinity, and the history of the grant from which it arose is interesting.

In the Ulster County Records[1] at Kingston is an indenture bearing date the 25th of August, 1709, signed by nine proprietors, eight of them Dutch and one of them a Huguenot, reciting that they had purchased, together with others, a "certaine tract of land near y$^e$ town of hürly afores$^d_:$," and extending south to the New Paltz patent. It refers to a patent of October 19, 1708, to "Cornelius Cool" and his associates, and goes on to say : that "whereas y$^e_:$ s$^d_:$ lands were more especially purchased & obtaÿned by y$^e$ parties in y$^e$ said deed & patent mentioned to serve as Commons for wood pasturage & drift[2] of Cattle to y$^e_:$ parties respectively in y$^e_:$ s$^d_:$ severall Instruments named . . . This Indenture wittnesseth . . . that upon y$^e_:$ decease of one or more of y$^e_:$ s$^d_:$ parties y$^e_:$ lands . . . shall not be subject to any survivorship but shall descend unto y$^e_:$ heirs of y$^e_:$ partie or parties respectively

---

were a people of French extraction and spoke the French language." Among the Walloons who came to New Netherland, about 1660, was this Louis DuBois, who played so prominent a part in the civil and religious life of the community which he did much to establish. He was born at Wicres in Flanders in 1627, went to the Palatinate about 1647, and was married at Mannheim in 1655. The name Wallkill, given to the stream whose rich border-lands attracted Louis DuBois, is by some derived from his traditional title of Louis the "Wall." Whether this be the origin of the name, or whether it came from the Holland branch of the Rhine called the Waal, this tributary of the Hudson serves, at all events, to emphasize that close relationship of the two Rhines which is elsewhere noted.

[1] Ulster County Records, Lib. AA. of Deeds, p. 494.

[2] This word "drift" in its use here is interesting because derived from the German *trift*, pasturage or drove; Anglo-Saxon, *drif*, a driving. It is a legitimate Teutonic representative of an old Teutonic custom.

as if y! same had been particularly divided . . . and it is further covenanted and agreed by y! parties aforesaid . . . y⁺ no part of y! s⁴ lands shall hereafter be divided but in such manner as in these pr⁰⁰cnts is exprest but y! y! wood lands shall for ever remain in common . . . and it is further covenanted and agreed . . . y⁺ in case it shall hereafter be thought reasonable to let sell or dispose of some small tract or tracts of arrable Land w⁰ʰ may happen in the s⁴ tract the same shall & may bee disposed for y! Common benefit by y! s⁴ parties or y! major part of them who are to execute y! necessary deeds for y! same, And it is further [agreed] that y! number of those that shall have anÿ right to dispose as afores⁴ shall bee nine or y! major part of them, and y⁺ how manÿ soever doe claime under any one of y! s⁴ purchazers . . . shall be only accounted as one & may appoint one of their number to vote for them all when any land is to be disposed of, And it is further covenanted & agreed between y! s⁴ parties that they . . . [shall not] sell or dispose of any of y! s⁴ wood lands to bee left in Common . . . to any person or persons not being an Inhabitant of y! town of horlÿ, arrable Lands Creekes for Mills and such like cases excepted and in case y! s⁴ Commons or any part thereof do by Inheritance or bÿ will descend or are bequeathed to any . . . not being an Inhabitant of y! s⁴ town he or they shall neverthelesse enjoy y! same but not sell y! same to any other . . . not being an Inhabitant . . . and it is further agreed y⁺ all monÿs to bee received for any arrable Lands bee alwaÿs divided amongst them and their heirs and assigns in nine equal shares or proportions." This exclusion from proprietorship of all who were not inhabitants of Hurley finds its prototype in the primitive mark of Germany, —notably where its organization has been preserved in the forest cantons of Switzerland. There " each inhabitant," says Laveleye, " owned his house and the adjacent plot as private property : the rest of the territory was collective property." Yet the general assembly or *Landesgemeinde,* " superintended the use of the forest and common pasture . . . and framed all necessary regulations. No one could sell his house or his land to a stranger."[1]

Ten years after the execution of the above agreement which sought to do away with survivorship-rights, and to fix forever the woodland as common property, an instrument[2] dated Sept. 3, 1719, under authority of the Governor and Assembly of the Colony, and signed by the Secretary, appointed seven of the Hurley freeholders as trustees of all the land included in the patent of 1708,[3] and, by incorporation, made them a body politic.[4] In case of vacancy in the board of trustees by death or disability, the freeholders and inhabitants were authorized to elect the successor by a majority of voices. They were also permitted to meet together in some public place annually the first Tuesday in April to elect "one or more Constables, Two or more Assessors, two or more Collectors one or more Supervisors and such and so many other town officers" as they should agree upon. To defray the expenses of procuring the Act of Confirmation from the Assembly the freeholders were to make payment "by voluntary and equal contributions." For the same purpose, however, the trustees were prudently given power to sell to the highest bidder any of the common lands within the tract, not to exceed the amount of £225 in value. The "succession as above Directed to be continued forever To and for the benefit and behoof of all the ffreeholders and inhabitants of the said town."

Apparently the "Hurley Commons" thus continued to be held for the public use by the locally appointed trustees, not,

---

[1] Laveleye, Prim. Prop., pp. 239–240.

[2] Town Clerk's Records, West Hurley.

[3] The patent mentioned before (p. 44), given to Cornelius Cool and associates, "to their heires and assignes forever," provided they settle and improve it within three years; "In ffree and common soccage as of our mannor of East Greenwich in the County of Kent." A rent of twelve shillings was reserved.

[4] Feudalism was asserted in the nominal yearly rent of one peppercorn, which the trustees had to pay to the Crown.

indeed, "forever," but for nearly a century;—until a division was " made in Pursuance of an Act of the Legislature of the State of New York entitled an Act for Dividing the Common Lands in the Town of Hurley in the County of Ulster passed the 4th of April 1806,"[1] three commissioners being duly appointed for the purpose. In the " Field Book " which contains the surveys and a record of the allotments made by the commissioners, is recited that portion of the act which specifies two classes who were to take part in the allotment, and it includes some of the inhabitants who had never had any rights, either by descent or purchase, in the original grant.

It provided,[2] "That there shall be set apart and conveyed to every Freeholder severally who shall own a Freehold within said Corporation of the Value of more than three hundred Dollars, and who shall reside therein at the time of passing this Act, and own and occupy a Dwelling House therein, one certain share or dividend of said Common Land, and where two or more persons are possessed of such Freehold as Joint tenants or tenants in common [they] shall be entitled to one such share and no more ; and to every Freeholder possessing a Freehold in said Corporation of the Value of less than three hundred Dollars and shall be a native thereof and shall own and occupy a Dwelling House therein at the time of passing this Act, a like share or Dividend of said Common Land which several Description of proprietors above mentioned shall be called the first Class. And be it further enacted, That there shall be set apart and conveyed to the following description of proprietors as a Second Class, viz : To every freeholder residing within the said Corporation at the time of psssing this Act and not being a native thereof, and possessing a Freehold therein of the value of less than three hundred Dollars, at (*sic*) who shall at the time of passing this Act, occupy a Dwelling House therein, one other

---

[1] Town Clerk's Recs., West Hurley, Field Book, p. 1.
[2] Town Clerk's Recs., West Hurley, Field Book, pp. 3, 4.

certain equal share or Dividend of the said Common Lands, not less than two thirds in Value of such share or dividend as shall be set apart for proprietors of the first Class ; And also a like two-thirds share or dividend to every inhabitant not being a Freeholder as shall have supported a family and resided within the said Corporation the term of two years next before making such partition and who shall during that term have followed some trade or occupation." The lots were to be as near the respective dwellings, and as nearly equal, as possible. Among those who were to be granted a lot of the first Class, were also non-resident owners of freehold of a value not less than two thousand dollars. The trustees were to settle all disputes, and to defray expenses by levying a tax on lots. They were given power to sell, after two years, the shares of those whose taxes were then unpaid. Under this act, the commissioners surveyed one hundred and sixty-eight lots, numbered regularly from 1 to 168, and Nov. 13, 1806, the allotment seems to have been made at the house of " Peter Elmendorf Inholder," the result being duly recorded in the Field Book.

This division of the common lands (both arable and woodland) at Hurley, in the first decade of the present century, presents features which call to mind the customs of the early Teutonic community, to-day surviving in some of the Rhine countries.[1] If it does not show a " periodic partition," it gives evidence of that distinctive feature of ancient communal landholding,—the reservation of a portion of the domain for "distribution among new families." To give to one who had been merely a resident (not a freeholder) of the town of Hurley two years, and had, during that time, " followed some

---

[1] Laveleye, Prim. Prop., p. 83. In speaking of the Allmends of Switzerland, he says : " In 1826, the commune of Pully-Petit put all its lands, previously divided, once more into community, and subjected them to a periodic partition among all the inhabitants every fifteen years, a part being reserved for distribution among new families." See also, Maine, Village Communities, pp. 81–87.

trade or occupation,"[1] a share in the allotment of land which had been granted a hundred years before to Cornelius Cool and associates, " to their heires and assignes forever," and which had been enjoyed during the century as the common territory of the freeholders of the town, is to establish the purely communal character of the tenure during that period. The distribution was made probably in compliance with a petition to the Legislature from the towns-people, and was based not, as were most of the partitions of the common lands along the Hudson about that time, upon hereditary rights in the domain, but upon the communistic theory of the needs of the individual residents; it was not *per stirpes*, but *per capita*. It was at once a readjustment of old titles and the conferring of entirely new ones.[2]

After this stride toward the holding of all lands in severalty, the freemen of Hurley still continued to meet in annual popular assembly to choose by majority vote " officers for the township of hurley,"—the seven trustees, town clerk, assessors, constables, collectors, overseers of the poor, commissioners of the highway, road-masters, and fence-viewers.[3]

The town of New Paltz, lying south of Hurley and the Esopus, also claims special attention. There, many of the peculiar characteristics of early village community-life appeared more distinctly, and continued for a longer time than in other towns along the river. To-day the quiet village is a station on the Wallkill Valley railroad, and one may reach it by

---

[1] Maine, Village Communities, p. 125. It is curious to note that Sir Henry Maine speaks of this provision for establishing trades as " yet another feature of the Indian cultivating groups which connects them with primitive western communities of the same kind."

[2] If it be asserted that this is only an incident of landlordship, that the nominal rent reserved kept the title in the sovereign, so that he might give the land to whomever he chose, the fact remains that freeholders who evidently supposed they held the land in fee, dealt with it in such a way as would best subserve the needs of the whole community.

[3] Town Clerk's Records, West Hurley, Town Records, 1793–1832.

steam from Kingston over a route, perhaps identical in part,
with that taken by the little band of slow-moving pioneer
settlers somewhat more than two hundred years ago. The
pleasanter way for one to gain his first impressions of New
Paltz, is to cross the Hudson from Poughkeepsie and drive
directly westward over an excellent turnpike ·road, lying
wholly within the territory of the original grant. Eight
miles from the river a point is reached which commands a
fine view of the surrounding country. In the north-west,
the Catskill peaks stand out boldly against the horizon ; and
in front, the nearer Shawangunk range stretches north and
south,—a natural barrier beyond which the early settler did
not venture. Sky Top, its most prominent point, marks the
location of Lake Mohonk,[1] and is the grand boundary stone
at the south-west corner of the New Paltz patent. Between
this ancient landmark and the view-point of the spectator, is
the valley of the Wallkill, whose cultivated fields present in
summer an appearance strikingly unusual. Almost everywhere the boundary lines seem to be rectangular, and the
fields, on the slope of the opposite mountain, sown with different kinds of grain or left as meadow land, look like the
regular blocks of a variegated patchwork. Just below, in
the valley, a mile away, on the east side of the stream, may
be seen the church steeples and scattered houses of New Paltz.
The road, entering the village from the east, becomes the main
street, and, on either side of it, nearly to the long covered
bridge by which it crosses the Wallkill, are the stores and
shops, constituting the local sources of supply for five or six
hundred inhabitants. The neat, unpretentious, dwellings
interspersed, are mostly modern, for this street did not become
the chief thoroughfare until long after the early settlement,
when the increasing agricultural population sought an outlet
for their produce by way of the Hudson river to New York.

---

[1] Spelled "Moggonck" in the Patent. In the Indian dialect it meant
"on the great sky top."

The streets running north and south, parallel to the stream, were the scenes of pioneer activity, and to-day one may discover, here and there, the steep-roofed houses of colonial times, one of which shows the old port holes, and displays in iron letters the date, 1705.

Tradition attributes the settlement at New Paltz to one of the incidents connected with the Indian massacre at Esopus in June, 1663. Catherine Blanshan, the wife of Louis DuBois, was one of the captives carried away into the wilderness. DuBois with a band of the settlers started in pursuit, and, in following the stream which was afterwards called the Wallkill, they noticed the rich lands in the vicinity of the present village of New Paltz. The search was successful, the prisoners were rescued from captivity, and in the more leisurely return to Esopus, Louis DuBois and his companions examined carefully the land which, by its beauty and apparent fertility, had before attracted their attention. Some years afterwards[1] he and his associates purchased from the Indians the large tract of land, estimated to contain some 36,000 acres, including part of the present townships of New Paltz, Rosendale, and Esopus, and the whole of Lloyd,—bounded on the west by the Shawangunk[2] mountains and on the east by the Hudson river. For this valuable grant the Indians received "40 kettles, 40 axes, 4 adzes, 40 shirts, 400 strings of white beads (wampum), 300 strings of black beads, 50 pairs of stockings, 100 bars of lead, 1 keg of powder, 100 knives, 4 quarter-casks of wine, 40 jars, 60 splitting or cleaving knives, 60 blankets, 100 needles, 100 awls, and 1 clean pipe."[3]

---

[1] May, 1677.

[2] This word is usually slurred in pronunciation so as to sound like *"Shongum."* Its meaning in the Indian dialect is somewhat doubtful. Rev. C. Scott, in an article on the subject (Collections of the Ulster Historical Society, I., pp. 229–33), suggests either "South Water," or the "Kill or Creek of the Shawanees."

[3] Ulster Co. Hist. (Everts & Peck, 1880), New Paltz, p. 5. The translation above given has been the generally accepted rendering of the Dutch words which represent the consideration for the grant. Rev. Ame Ven-

This purchase was soon confirmed by a patent signed by Gov. Andross, dated Sept. 29, 1677, granting to "Louis DuBois and partners," the land described, for the yearly rent of "five Bushels of good Winter wheat." The instrument now in the Huguenot Bank at New Paltz, names the twelve patentees as follows : " Louis DuBois, Christian Doyo, Abraham Haesbroocq Andries Lefevre, Joan Broocq Pierre Doyo, Laurens Bivere Anthony Crospell, Abraham DuBois, Hugo Frere Isaack DuBois and Symeon LeFevre, their heyres and Assignes." All were Huguenots, who fleeing from kingly and church persecution in France, had found an asylum in the Lower Palatinate at Mannheim, and had probably spent some time in Holland also, whence they had come with the Dutch to Esopus. In memory of their German home on the banks of the Rhine and adjacent to the forest region of the Odenwald, they named their new home on the Hudson, New Paltz,[1] or the New Palatinate, and here established, to a considerable degree, the local government and peculiar customs of the German village community.

Local history asserts that "as soon as these hardy pioneers had established themselves upon their lands they proceeded to make an equitable division of them. This was done in a rude way, each family portion being measured off by paces and staked at the corners. These boundaries were never changed ; but to these tracts were given special names, such as Pashemoy, Pashecanse, Wicon, Avenyear, Lanteur, Granpere, etc., which have survived two hundred years. The lands were at first tilled in Common and the proceeds equally divided."[2]

---

nema, of New Paltz, who has recently given the subject attention, is inclined to think the Dutch word "*Zeewandt,*" which has been usually translated "beads" (the white ones being used for wampum), should be rendered, "400 fathoms of material used for fish nets." He also reads, "40 oars," instead of "40 jars;" "60 pieces of duffel" (coarse woolen cloth), instead of "60 cleaving knives"; and "1 measure of tobacco," instead of "1 clean pipe."

[1] Sometimes spelled "Pals" in the early records; German, Pfalz.

[2] Ulster County History (Everts & Peck, 1880), New Paltz, p. 6. See Edmund Eltinge, Colls. Ulster Hist. Soc., Vol. I., Part 1, p. 47.

Perhaps no documents now exist which establish the evidence of this early cultivation in common of tracts of the
arable land by the numerous co-owners, but tradition, both
trustworthy and direct, places the matter almost beyond
question. One of the worthy representatives of her Huguenot
ancestors told the writer a few weeks ago that in her younger
days she used frequently to hear an old resident of New Paltz
relate how his mother, a self-reliant, vigorous woman, was
wont, after becoming a widow, to take her turn in caring for
the common stock and crops, as her husband had done before.
The small tracts thus cultivated in common were doubtless
the choicest portions of the land near the Wallkill, in which
all the inhabitants desired to have some share. Each year
the co-owners determined what crops should be planted, and
chose some one of their number to care for the interests of all.
If there are no early documents to verify this tradition of a
common cultivation and division of the produce, there are
those which intimate a common ownership even in the arable
land, and show conclusively such common rights in both
pasture and woodland as are thoroughly characteristic everywhere of Teutonic village community-life.

In a will of Louis DuBois, dated March 30, 1686,[1] it is
provided in reference to New Paltz land that "them that
have home lotts and have built thereon shall keep the same—
upon condition that the other of my children shall have so
much land instead thereof in such convenient places as may
be found most expedient for them in any place belonging to
my said estate."[2]

A deed[3] in 1705, by Anthony Crespel, one of the patentees of the New Paltz, recites that he "Lawfully standeth
seized and possest of $y^e$ twelfth part of the whole pattent of
$y^e$ New paltz as by said patent" etc., and gives for divers

---

[1] There were two later wills.

[2] Ulster County Clerk's Office Records, Liber of Deeds, AA., p. 49.

[3] Ulster County Clerk's Office Records, Liber of Deeds, AA., p. 386.

considerations to his daughter, "Severall lotts parcels and pieces of y$^e$ above said part of land of the new paltz," one lot being described as "between a lott of Abraham dü boÿs and the Commons . . . Also the Just third part of y$^e$ woods & Commons of y$^e$ above & first mentioned twelfth part of land of s$^d$ Crespel that is nott y$^eu$ laÿd out and devided." It then provides that the land shall not "bee disposed of to strangers,"[1] but gives full power to the children "to sell convey and sett over their respective parts and proportions of the above s$^d$ parcells and lotts of land unto anÿ of y$^e$ family in blood of the said Anthony Crespel." In the so-called "New Paltz Orders,"[2] the fencing of the common lands seems to include land not for pasturage, and presumably arable land. It is thus provided for in popular assembly : "We the inhabitants of y$^e$ Niew Pals in generall are met to-gether y$^e$ 23$^{th}$ day of Feb. 17$\frac{1}{12}$ to conclued concerning all our fences of the Land as also of the pastures to the plurality of votes according to the order of the warrant to the constable directed : . . . the N. Pals town shall to-gether make the fence from Jacob Hasbroucq, to the s$^d$ gate, and so we shall begin the vasmakerslant[3] fences to the kill or kreek at the Landing place, to the erf[4] of John Hasbroucq and every one of us must make his part or share at six Raeles as now is . . . More concerning the old pastures every one is obliged and bound to doe as his nebourgh that is to say the just half of y$^e$ fences of five Raels or otherwise & that good and sufficient. And as for y$^e$ kettel doing Dammage and so taken they shall be put in pound by him that shall thereunto be chosen or impoured by the inhabitants of s$^d$ place. And each and every horse or cow beast so taken

---

[1] The same exclusive provision which prevailed at Hurley. See p. 45.

[2] Records in Huguenot Bank at New Paltz.

[3] The meaning of this word is doubtful. The spelling is probably faulty.

[4] "Erf" means "inheritance," and in its use here shows that probably the Dutch spoke of the "home lot" as such, in distinction from the common lands. It is suggestive at least.

in dammage shall pay a peace nine pence for a fine, the one half for him there-unto chosen and the other half for the Towne. And as for the hogs they shall have no Liberties for to Runne free ; but as for the sheeps they may runne free untill that time that they goe in Dammage in y° Corne or in the pastures provided y° fences be good and sufficient . . . And as for the horses which Rune upon the Land in the fale they shall be taken away the 30th of September . . . Concerning all the fences[1] . . . each and every one is oblidged and bound to make and kepe his owne fence at the time Limitted or ordered by him thereunto chosen to take notice of s<sup>d</sup> fences, but in case any one neglict or will not doe or make his fence he shall pay for a fine six shillings, and the viewers of fences shall make or have made the s<sup>d</sup> fence or fences at his own charge as y° Law Direct in such case." The " Orders " also imposed, upon any one leaving gates open, fines to pay the " cost and charges of the towne," and were recorded by " W. Nottingham Clerk."

The patentees are said to have been called the " Twelve Men " or " Duzine," and to have had both legislative and judicial powers in town affairs. Three years before the death of the surviving patentee, Abraham, son of Louis Du Bois, the twenty-four proprietors of the New Paltz entered into an agreement[2] dated April 21, 1728, which established the local government of the " Twelve Men " by popular election, and authorized them to fix titles " according to the severall Divisions and partitions that have been made between them [the patentees] by Parole without deed, and the other parts thereof yet remaining in common and undivided . . . within the bounds of the aforesaid Pattent." It states that, " we Doe by

---

[1] It is interesting to compare these " New Paltz Orders " relating to the ancient institution, the " Common Fence," with the evidences of similar customs in New England, collected by Dr. Adams in his " Germanic Origin of New England Towns."—" Studies," I., p. 32 of monograph just mentioned.

[2] Records in Huguenot Bank at New Paltz.

these presents Covenant and Grant to and with each other that there shall and may be yearly and every year for ever, hereafter chosen and elected for the purposes above mentioned by the plurality votes of the ffreeholders and Inhabitants within the aforesaid Pattent Twelve good able and sufficient men ffreeholders and Inhabitants who have an Interest within the said pattent Representing the aforesaid Twelve Pattentees."

. . . Further we " Give Grant and Bequeath unto the aforesaid Twelve men or the Major part of them to be elected and nominated in manner as aforesaid full power and authority to act and sett in good order and unity all common affairs—Businesses or things Comeing before them belonging to or concerning the Right Title Interest or property of the Township of the New Paltz aforesaid and commonalty within the said Pattent according to Law or Equity and to the best of their knowledge and understanding." Then follows a covenant to pay all charges disbursed by the " Twelve Men " for defending title, and giving deeds of partitions made by the twelve patentees in their life time. Full power is also given them to make partition of undivided land, "as they shall from time to time see cause for : . . which Division is to be made in manner and forme following That is to say that the said Undivided Lands and premises, or such part thereof as they shall from time to time see cause for . . . shall be laid out in Twelve equal shares and Divisions soe that the one is not of more vallue than the other and Then the aforesaid Twelve shares or Divisions shall be numbered and then the aforesaid Twelve men shall Draw Lotts for the same," each share in the allotment to be for the use of those who represent, by descent or otherwise, the several patentees. The " Twelve Men " were empowered to give deeds for the parcels, and such conveyances were to remain forever.

The character of the rights of commonage then enjoyed at New Paltz is well shown by a release[1] in the following year

---

[1] Now in possession of Edmund Eltinge, Esq.

(Apr. 5, 1729), from the "Twelve Men" granting to Solomon and Louis DuBois and their heirs "full power and authority at all times forever hereafter to cut down, load have take and carry away all manner of Timber trees and stones standing . . . lying and being within any part of the Commons and without the ffences and inclosures of any of the Inhabitants of the new paltz aforesaid in the same manner that the said owners and proprietors Doe use to Doe in the said Commons, and likewise to mow down and carry away any grass or hay growing without the ffences and inclosures and in the Commons[1] . . . [under] such regulations as the owners and proprietors aforesaid in the said town cut hay in the Commons, to-geather with free liberty of ingress, egress and regress to and for the said Solomon Dubois and Lewis Dubois and their heirs or assignes " . . . Provided always, "that they shall have no similar rights in inclosed lands nor take anything they may rightfully take in the uninclosed lands for any person outside of their ffour ffamilys liveing on the said tract of land of the said Solomon Dubois and Lewis Dubois."

The "Twelve Men" under their authority, conferred in the agreement of 1728, to lay out the land to be divided "in Twelve equal shares and Divisions soe that the one is not of more vallue than the other," had the lots set off regularly from time to time, of the same size and shape, adjacent and numbered from 1 to 12 in each Division,—the North and South Divisions together constituting one long strip (or Tier) of similar lots, running for the most part north and south, parallel to the Wallkill.[2] Almost all deeds of New Paltz property, executed after the signing of the agreement of 1728 and before the general partition of the lands by the State legis-

---

[1] In connection with these rights of commonage we find the ancient Pound. In 1765 one of the questions put to the voters of New Paltz was "whether Poundmasters shall be elected or every man be his own Pounder."

[2] In such regular division of the territory by the "Twelve Men," may be found an explanation of the rectangular boundary lines which strike the eye of one who approaches New Paltz from the east.

lature at the beginning of the present century, contain reference to this method of division.  In one dated April 3, 1767,
given by Noah Eltinge to Josiah Eltinge, the land is described
as " on the east side of the Paltz River being . . . known by
Lot number three, situate in the first twelve Lots or South
Division of the New Division called the First Tier, lying
eastward of the old Divisions on the east side of the Paltz
River and adjacent thereunto."[1]  One third part of one hundred and eighty acres was granted.

A will[2] of Roeloff Eltinge, dated 1745, gives among other
bequests the half part of his share in sundry " Lotts of Land.'
laid out within the Limitts of the Pattent of the new Paltz
afores<sup>d</sup> fronting upon hudsons River and extending westerly
from the said River one mile & a half."  In this same will
there is evidence, not only that between the Tiers of divided
lands large tracts lay undivided and owned in common, but
also, that before the middle of the last century the shares in
such common land were becoming minutely subdivided.  The
testator bequeathed to his son Noah all his " farme Lands
meadows " etc., in the New Paltz, " and also all that the one
third part of the one sixth and one sixtieth part of all the
undivided Land within the Bounds of the Pattent of the New
Paltz afores<sup>d</sup>."

Thirty years later, and nearly a hundred years after the
granting of the patent, fifty-two proprietors of the New Paltz
entered into an agreement,[3] dated April 30, 1774, for the
common defence of their territory,—a fact which shows the per-

---

[1] Doc. in possession of Jacob Elting, Esq.

[2] Document now in possession of Jacob Elting, Esq.

[3] Records in Huguenot Bank at New Paltz.  There is also an earlier
agreement, dated May 23, 1744, by which the signers pledge themselves,
under heavy penalty, " To Defend Joyntly the whole Tract . . . and to
stand in mutual Defence of each other Lot or Lots Farm and Farms against
all Incroachments and Pretences of Right To the lands forever . . . For
Fifteen whole and consecutive years."  The " Twelve Men " were to determine the amount of money needed.

sistence of their village community customs and the extent to which the subdivision of the common property had then been carried. The agreement recites the patent of 1677, and the articles of 1728 by which the "Twelve Men" had been permanently established, and then goes on to say : "That each and every one of us whose hands and seals are hereunto set and our respective Heirs and Assigns, shall and will advance, disburse and Pay unto the said twelve Men for the time being or to the Major Part of them, such a proportionable part of the said common stock as we respectively have here-under annexed to our several and respective names and that as many times and as often as it shall be requisite and necessary for the defending the said Tract of Land, or any part thereof." It was stipulated that the major part of the "Twelve Men" should settle disputes as to what were necessary disbursements, and the proprietors bound themselves to the "Twelve Men" "in the Penal sum of Two Hundred Pounds current Money of New York." Among the fifty-two who signed were :

| | | | |
|---|---|---|---|
| Daniel Lefever | $\frac{6}{14}$ part, | Benjamin I. Freer | $\frac{2}{14}$ part, |
| Jacob Louw | $\frac{7}{158}$ " , | Jacobus Hasbrouck | $\frac{8}{15}$ " , |
| Anthony Yelverton | $\frac{3}{12}$ " , | Josia Eltinge | $\frac{7}{150}$ parts, |
| And⁸ Bevier | $\frac{10}{53}$ " , | Noach Eltinge | $\frac{1}{17}$ part, |
| Jonas Hasbrouck | $\frac{1}{120}$ " , | Abraham doiau | $\frac{6,7}{120}$ parts. |

Much discussion was provoked concerning the validity of the above agreement, and, as is so often the case, the prominent lawyers consulted differed in opinion. Egbert Benson, Oct. 5, 1791, asserted that " it is wholly incompetent to the purposes for which it was intended,"[1]—that is, to bind the shares of the land in perpetuity to a proportional contribution. Earlier in the same year John Addison had advised the "Twelve Men" " that the Instrument is valid in Law, and the sums all recoverable."[2] This was also the opinion of Clinton. That the agreement was still in force twenty-

---

[1] Records in the Huguenot Bank at New Paltz.
[2] Records in the Huguenot Bank at New Paltz.

four years after its execution, is shown by an entry of May 23, 1798, in the book of the "Twelve Men" containing the records of their transactions: "It is agreed by the Majority of the Twelve Men . . . to Rase the sum of Two Hundred Pounds for and Towards Defending the Bounderies of the New paltz Pattent and the proportion of each man is affixed oposite to his name to Base the above mentioned sum and each Twelve man is to collect his proportion of the sum and pay it to the Twelve Men on or before the fifteenth day of August next."[1]

For more than a hundred years, the "Twelve Men" or. "Duzine" of New Paltz, had practically constituted the only legislative and judicial tribunal of the village. No doubt an appeal lay to the colonial government, but, so far as is known, none seems to have been taken. From 1677 to 1785, the "Common Book" of the "Duzine" contained the most important village records. In March of the latter year, an act[2] of the legislature incorporated the township under the state government, and confirmed the grants and partitions of the "Twelve Men."[3] But apparently the freeholders of New Paltz still continued to elect each year, as before, their "Twelve Men" for the supervision of local affairs,[4]

---

[1] Records in the Huguenot Bank at New Paltz.

[2] An "exemplification" of this act is among the records of the town now in the Huguenot Bank. The act provided that those taking by lot under the partition "shall be deemed . . . to have been seized severally in fee simple of the said Lots, or parcels of Land respectively;" and it adds that "the partition hereby confirmed shall be deemed and adjudged to be as good evidence of an estate in severalty under the said Paltz Patent as if such partition had been made according to the course of the Common Law." There seems to be no record at New Paltz, as there is at Hurley, of provision being made, in the partition of the common territory, for such of the inhabitants as had never before been freeholders.

[3] An advertisement of partition by the commissioners appeared in the Albany Gazette, Aug. 9, 1792.

[4] Though, after the incorporation of the town, the "Twelve Men" had little else to do than to determine the land-titles of the town and preserve the records of previous divisions.

even into the present century. The last record in the
Book of the Twelve Men tells us that, as late as April,
1824, "At the annual Townmeeting of the freeholders and
Inhabitants of the Town of New Paltz on the first tuesday
of April 1824 the following persons were chosen and elected
by plurality of votes of the freeholders & inhabitants of the
patent of New paltz for twelve men by Virtue & in persu-
ence of a certain instrument in writing made for that purpose." The record also names the chosen representatives,
designating for each, respectively, the share of some one of the
original patentees. One of the "Twelve Men" elected at this
time was Daniel DuBois, who had been chosen to the same office
for the four preceding years. By members of his family, the
papers of the "Twelve Men," now in the Huguenot Bank,
were brought to "a meeting held at the house of Benjamin
D. Smedes on the 3rd day of Apr. 1858 of the Inhabitants
of the town New Paltz persuant to public notice," for the
purpose of choosing a custodian for the documents of "the
Twelve." [1] These facts would seem to indicate that Daniel
DuBois, who lived until thirty-three years ago (March 15,
1852), was the last survivor [2] of the last "Duzine;" and thus
he might have claimed the unique distinction of perpetuating
in his own person, as late as the middle of the 19th century, an
institution older than the Christian era.

No account of the town of New Paltz would be complete,
if it did not make some mention of the marked character
of the religious life which produced, side by side with so
interesting a civil organization, a noteworthy church establishment. When the Indians were overtaken by Louis

---

[1] The meeting "Resolved that the patent papers be kept and held by
Methusalem Eltinge. Ab$^m$ P. Lefever Pres.——Ab$^m$ H. Deyo Jr. Sec."

[2] Dr. Peltz, however, in an address at the DuBois Reunion in 1875, says:
"One gentleman sits before me to-day who has been chosen the representative of his tribe." Query: Did he refer to Ab$^m$ P. Lefever, who was
president of the above mentioned meeting, and who did not die till 1879?
The records, however, do not show his election as one of the "Twelve Men."

DuBois and his band, in that journey which included the discovery of the New Paltz lands, the captive women were staying the hands of the savages by singing the 137th psalm;[1] and more than a dozen years afterward when the little group of Huguenot settlers, who had left their Dutch friends at the Esopus, reached the *Tri-Cor*[2] near the present village of New Paltz, one of the number read from the French Bible the 23rd psalm, and then led the company in prayer.

After their settlement, almost at once, the community erected a rough log house to serve both for school and church.[3] These Huguenot pioneers at New Paltz, having been driven from France to the Palatinate in Germany, as a temporary asylum from the fires of persecution which were everywhere lighted in France, even before the formal Revocation of the Edict of Nantes, brought with them to their " new Palatinate " that fervor of religious life born only of martyrdom,—a fervor quite as strong as, and more tolerant than, that which inspired the early settlers of New England. It is not strange, therefore, that within six years the Huguenots at New Paltz obtained a minister, the Rev. Pierre Daillie,

---

[1] This interesting episode has been commemorated by Edmund Eltinge, Esq., of New Paltz, in a large historical oil painting now in his possession, which he had painted for him by a skilful artist over thirty years ago. In the foreground are the captive women near a group of Indians, and on the right, just emerging from the woods, are Louis DuBois and his Huguenot companions, dressed in the costume of their day, advancing from the thicket with their guns to put the Indians to flight. In the back-ground, beyond the Wallkill Valley, is the Shawangunk range with its prominent point, " Sky Top," strongly defined against the horizon ; and further in the distance, to the north, is a glimpse of the Catskills. The rich autumn foliage of the region is well put upon the canvas, and, altogether, the painting is a noteworthy representation of this memorable incident in the early pioneer life of the New Paltz settlers.

[2] *Tri-Cor* refers to the *three cars*, or wagons, in which the settlers had brought their worldly goods.

[3] The Dutch had in their early charters to the West India Company provided for both schoolmaster and minister in the Hudson river settlements, and the Huguenots showed themselves equally zealous in the cause of education and religion.

"and formed themselves into a congregation by the name of
the Walloon Protestant Church, after the manner and discipline of the Church of Geneva." [1]  The first record of this
church organization is interesting.  It is in French, and the
following translation of a portion shows that the popular
methods of government which marked the civil life of the
community, prevailed thus early also in their church establishment: "The 22nd of January, 1683, Mr. Pierre Daillie,
minister of the Word of God, arrived in New Paltz and
preached twice on the following Sunday, and proposed to the
heads of the families that they should choose by majority of
votes, by the fathers of families, one Elder and one deacon,
which they did, and chose Louis DuBois for elder and Hugh
Frere for deacon to assist the minister in guiding the members of the church that meets in New Paltz;" [2]

This *l'eglise de Nouveau Palatinat*, as it was early called,
is probably the only church in America whose records are
written successively in three languages, each period illustrating a different epoch in the church life and government.
Approximately, they may be said to have been kept fifty
years in French, seventy in Dutch, and since the beginning
of this century in English.  Within twenty years after the
election of the first church officers, the records appear to have
been partly in Dutch, and this language was chiefly in use
throughout the eighteenth century,—a fact which shows the
dominating character of Dutch influence in colonial New
York, even in a settlement which, like New Paltz, was at first
entirely Huguenot.

In marked contrast with the religious intolerance of the
New England colonists, was the broad Christian liberality of
the Dutch and Huguenots who laid the foundations of New
York State.  Often, when their own French church was without a pastor, the Huguenot settlers of the New Paltz went

<hr>

[1] Hasbrouck MS.  See "Life and Times of Louis DuBois," by Anson
DuBois, DuBois Reunion 1876, Proceedings, p. 67.
[2] See Fac-simile of Record, DuBois Reunion, 1876, Proceedings, pp. 8, 9.

with their Dutch friends to the Dutch church at Kingston to attend the communion service, or to have the right of baptism administered to their children;[1] and, in turn, the increasing Dutch population at New Paltz not only worshipped in the French church of the Huguenots, but even acted as its officers and wrote its records in their native language. In this transition period of life and language, from French to Dutch, the ministers, it is likely, were frequently called upon to give alternate discourses in the two languages,[2] as it is certain they gave them in Dutch and English, during the later transition at the close of the last century.

So close, indeed, was the agreement between the Huguenots and the Dutch at New Paltz, that we find the former, although they had been accustomed to a more independent church government, joining those of the Dutch, who, in the sharp controversy between the *Coetus* and *Conferentia* parties, held with the Conferentia faction that their ministers must be ordained in Holland by the classis of Amsterdam. Thus the French Reformed Church of the early settlers merged into the Dutch Reformed Church of New Paltz, which to-day stands as the exponent in the community of a religious life that gained much of its original strength under French and Spanish persecutions. In New York, as in New England, the desire for religious freedom accompanied and inspired the persistent purpose to obtain popular local self-government, which made possible the formation of our United States.

Having examined, somewhat in detail, many marked types of village community government in New Netherland and New York, one may well pause to consider the precise signifi-

---

[1] In the early settlements of New Amsterdam, some seventy or eighty years before the time with which we are dealing, "for many years Huguenot and Dutch worshiped together."—Proceedings of Huguenot Society of America, I., p. 27.

[2] In a French will of 1730, there is a gift of a Bible, to go to the church, for the reading of the *French* service. The will is an eminently religious document, and by it the maker bequeaths everything to " *'eglise du nouveau pals.*"

cance of the bond of union which thus brings together the Rhine and the Hudson into close institutional relationship,— a relationship closer perhaps than even that between Old England and New England. ( It should be noted in the first place that the Hudson river towns may properly be spoken of as *Dutch* village communities, although only fifty years under Dutch rule, and composed in part of emigrants from France, Germany, and Great Britain. ) A writer,[1] as late as 1750, says that more than half of the inhabitants of New York were Dutch, and not until the close of the last century did Dutch give way to English as the prevailing language among the people.[2] Dutch manners and customs, Dutch forms of government, civil and ecclesiastical, prevailed not only in the early settlements, but persisted and remained dominant long after English rule supplanted that of Holland.

These outward forms of Dutch influence in early New York are interesting chiefly as exponents of the character of the colonists. It was the spirit of the people of the United Netherlands, which in the Fatherland had, through centuries, kept the feudal system from gaining there the foothold it obtained in France and England, and had at last thrown off the Spanish yoke,—it was this spirit which, prevailing in the colonies along the Hudson river, contended persistently for the rights of popular representative government, until they were attained in the General Assembly of 1664, just at the downfall of the Dutch West India Company's monopoly, and which again, after twenty years of arbitrary English rule, forced from an unwilling government the Representative Assembly of 1683.

---

[1] Rev. Mr. Burnaby (1750), Valentine's History of N. Y. City, p. 296.

[2] The long prevalence of the Dutch language, which has been noted in the New Paltz church records, was not merely local, but general throughout the colony. Smith, in his History of New York, writing in 1756, (more than ninety years after the first English possession,) says that "the sheriffs find it difficult to obtain persons sufficiently acquainted with the English tongue to serve as jurors in the Courts of law."

If one traces the origin and growth of this liberty-loving sentiment of the Dutch people, one is carried back to the earliest ages of north European history,—to a time, a century or more before the Christian era, when a hardy race called by Cæsar, the Menapii, occupied the country between the Rhine and the Meuse, and the Schelde and the ocean.[1] They (the Menapii) " held alliance with the Romans, *but never submitted to their yoke at all nor permitted them to introduce their language,* but retained in perpetual use the Teutonic (Theotiscam) dialect, now Dutch. Therefore, on this account, they called themselves Franci (Free Men) from the liberty they enjoyed.[2] These early inhabitants of the Netherlands seem to have been not only *free-men,* but also, as their name imports, (it being derived from two German words *MEEN—AFFT,* Dutch, Gemeen-Schap,) a community of nations or a confederation.[3] If this be so, one may trace from this earliest alliance of independent Teutonic tribes, those ideas of government which, sixteen hundred years later (in 1579), were embodied in the union of Utrecht; and, in turn, from this more recent confederation of States in the Netherlands, one may derive by a continuous race-tradition, through the Dutch village communities on the Hudson river, that principle of the union of sovereign powers which gave form to our United States.[4]

---

[1] Gen. J. Watts de Peyster, Netherlanders, p. 23.
[2] Gen. J. Watts de Peyster, Netherlanders, p. 19.
[3] Gen. J. Watts de Peyster, Netherlanders, p. 24.
He cites many authorities and among them Olivarius Vredius Brugis Flandorum apud Joannem Baptistam Kerchovium . . . Anno 1639.
[4] Brodhead, History of New York, p. 362, bears out this theory of the influence of Teutonic example by stating that the doctrine of States Rights is three centuries old, and by asserting that "The Union of Utrecht . . . was essentially the model for the first union of American Colonies." He even explains on the same theory, the confederation of the New England Colonies against the Dutch and the Indians in 1643, and notes that the Plymouth immigrants had learned valuable lessons in constitutional liberty during a twelve years sojourn in Holland. However that may be, it is certain that the Puritans have as little right to claim originality in establishing a confederacy, as in using the venerable town-meeting for the management

Special evidence of the close relationship between the free institutions of the Rhine and the Hudson is furnished by the village of New Paltz. The first proprietors were all Huguenots,—DuBoises, LeFevres, Deyos, Freres, and Hasbroucks, who, fleeing from France, had escaped the oppression both of the church and of the feudal system, and had probably gained familiarity with the free village community government, afterwards established here, during their residence on the banks of the Rhine in the German Palatinate,[1] where to-day, in the clearings of the adjacent Odenwald, are to be found almost perfect types of the primitive Germanic mark.

Yet another tie binds New Paltz and her local institutions to the old world. Only fifteen years was the "New Palatinate" a purely Huguenot community. As early as 1703, the Dutch element was introduced in the person of Roeloff Eltinge upon his marriage with Sarah DuBois, and thereafter the Eltings (and to a less degree other Dutch families) became prominent in the affairs of the township; so much so, indeed, that seventy years later, one member of the family—Noah Elting—owned one-seventeenth of all the common and undivided territory of the original grant. It is a curious and

---

of their local affairs. Both were Teutonic heritages reaching America from Holland and Germany directly, by a purer line of descent, than from England, which, to carry out the figure, may be called a relative of the *half blood.* How strong the influence of Holland and Germany was, in shaping the growth of our country, must be apparent to any careful reader of the events just prior to the Revolution. Not only in New York, but elsewhere in the colonies, patriotic minds were impressed by "the Helvetic Confederacy and the States of the United Netherlands as glorious examples of what 'a petty people in comparison' could do when acting together in the cause of liberty." Frothingham, Rise of the Republic of the United States, p. 199; quoting Richard Bland of Virginia (1766).

"United States," as a legal term, it is interesting to note, dates from Monday, Sept. 9, 1776, when Congress "Resolved, That in all Continental Commissions and other instruments, where, heretofore, the words 'United Colonies' have been used, the stile be altered, for the future, to the 'United States.'" Journals of Congress, Vol. I., p. 470. The expression had before been used in the Declaration of Independence.

[1] Conf. Fiske, American Pol. Ideas, p. 52.

interesting fact that Jan Eltinge [1]—the father of the first
New Paltz freeholder Roeloff—was, as is shown by his certifi-
cate of church membership,[2] born in 1632 at Beyle, in the
province of Drenthe in Holland; in which, says Laveleye,
"the Germanic *mark* still exists; . . . surrounded on all
sides by marsh and bog, this province formed a kind of island
of sand and heath, on which ancestral customs were preserved
in their entirety. Even in our day we find the ancient organization of the Saxon *mark;*"[3] De Amicis, also, in his recent
work on "Holland and Its People," speaking of Drenthe,
says: "Every thing in this strange province is antique and
mysterious. The customs of primitive Germany are found
here, tillage of the ground is common on the *Esschen*, the
rustic horn calling the peasants to labor, the houses described
by Roman historians, and over all this ancient world the
perpetual mystery of an immense silence."[4]

It is not strange, therefore, that in New Paltz the union of
the Huguenots and the Dutch, who had brought the forms of
primitive local government from two such sources as the forest
regions of the Odenwald and the marshy peat fields of
Drenthe, should result in a continuance of ancient village
community customs here on the Hudson river, even into the
present century.

From the banks of the Rhine, the germs of free local institutions, borne on the tide of western emigration, found here,.
along the Hudson, a more fruitful soil than New England
afforded for the growth of those forms of municipal, state,
and national government, which have made the United States
the leading Republic among the nations.

Thus in a new, and historically important sense, may the
Hudson river be called the "Rhine of America."

---

[1] He was a magistrate at Hurley, in 1683.
[2] Colls. Ulster Hist. Society, Vol I., Part 2, p. 177. The original certifi-
cate is in the possession of Edmund Eltinge, Esq.
[3] Laveleye, Prim. Prop., p. 282.
[4] De Amicis, Holland and its People, p. 390.